"I AIN'T COMIN' BACK!"

John Wearn
Pro 3:5-6

"I AIN'T COMIN' BACK"

DOLPHUS WEARY
AND WILLIAM HENDRICKS

Tyndale House Publishers, Inc.
Wheaton, Illinois

Special Printing, 1997

Unless otherwise noted, Scripture quotations are taken from
the *Holy Bible,* The New King James Version. Copyright
© 1979, 1980, 1982, Thomas Nelson Inc., Publishers.

Scripture quotations marked NIV are from the *Holy Bible,*
New International Version. Copyright © 1973, 1978, 1984
International Bible Society. Used by permission of
Zondervan Bible Publishers.

Scripture quotations marked TLB are taken from *The Living
Bible,* copyright © 1971 owned by assignment by KNT
Charitable Trust. All rights reserved.

Front cover illustration copyright © 1990 Bob Fuller

Library of Congress Catalog Card Number 90-70607
ISBN 0-8423-1609-4
Copyright © 1990 by Dolphus Weary and The Mendenhall
Ministries, Inc.
All rights reserved
Printed in the United States of America

97
8   7

This book is dedicated to my family: my wife, Rosie, whose love, loyalty, and support have been constant throughout my years; and my children, Danita, Reggie, and Ryan, who willingly share my time with the ministry. It is also dedicated to the Mendenhall Bible Church/Mendenhall Ministries family.

Proceeds from the sell of this book are used to fund a rural Christian foundation which will help build Christian leaders for years to come.

CONTENTS

ACKNOWLEDGMENTS

This book has been completed by the grace of God. He has orches-trated many hands that have touched this book in ways known and unknown in order to put it into your hands. I want to mention a few individuals who deserve extra special thanks:

John Perkins, my spiritual dad, has meant a lot to me over the years. As I formulated a vision for Mendenhall Ministries, he helped to shape that vision.

Artis Fletcher, the pastor of Mendenhall Bible Church, has en-couraged me and stood with me for many years. He has been a true partner with me in the development of this ministry.

Jimmie Walker and I broke new ground at school together and spent time dreaming and working together here at Mendenhall.

Matthew Parker came to our aid in 1979 and has walked beside us since as we laid the groundwork for presenting Mendenhall Minis-tries publicly. He was generous in using his considerable network of contacts on our behalf.

C. J. Jones came to the ministry at a very critical time in our devel-opment when we needed his organizational, planning, and manage-ment skills.

Alice Wigden spent many hours retyping various pieces of the manuscript, editing my remarks, and helping me clarify my thoughts for the printed page.

Bill Berry walked beside us in the process of bringing the book to the attention of several publishers, and ultimately under the care of Tyndale House.

Kevin Lake encouraged me to write this book from 1979 on. Many thanks to Dr. Lake, who has served as a Mendenhall Minis-tries board member since 1983.

Guy Parker's story—of a native Mississippian who grew up on the "right" side of the tracks and learned reconciliation toward us—has meant very much to me.

So much of the success of Dolphus Weary and Mendenhall Minis-tries is also the product of all of those young people with whom we have ministered since 1971.

The staff and Board of Directors of Mendenhall Ministries, the body of Mendenhall Bible Church, and innumerable friends have also been warm and positive in their expressions to me about this book.

Finally, I deeply appreciate the many organizations that have used Mendenhall Ministries as a model for their own work, at least in part. I particularly want to praise Wayne Gordon at Lawndale Community Church in Chicago and Kathy Dudley of Voice of Hope Ministries in Dallas.

SPECIAL THANKS

I'm deeply indebted to Chris Erb, who at her own expense travelled from Massachusetts to Mendenhall several times in order to tape conversations with my mother and others who have known me for years. She took those tapes home and, after transcribing them, spent many hours editing the material into a first manuscript.

Chris was the ministry's first volunteer, beginning in 1969, and came each summer for the next seven or eight summers. She had enough faith to believe that there was a book here in Mendenhall, and her early work in pulling a preliminary manuscript out of me was superb.

Bea Shira also deserves special recognition because she spent the time needed to get the original manuscript into readable form. That meant lots of tedious hours rewriting, rereading, and corresponding with me about details.

I met Bea at Second Presbyterian Church in Memphis, Tennessee. She had edited books and articles for a number of publishing companies, and she believed that my story was worth telling. Without her encouragement and labor of love, this book might still be unfinished.

Finally, Bill Hendricks proved to be my guardian angel in this publication process. He spent immeasurable time talking with me, taping me, transcribing the tapes, and editing long, arduous conversations from which he pulled out the details that make this book live.

Bill made a commitment to me to use his skills, abilities, and finances in order to deliver a manuscript that would be acceptable for publication. He has built this book into what it is.

Dolphus Weary
Mendenhall, Mississippi
February 1990

FOREWORD
BY JOHN PERKINS

Dolphus Weary's book rekindled mixed emotions in me—both the love and the hate that I have for Mississippi. It also made me realize again how the power of love can change and stabilize one's life.

Dolphus's years of growing up were much like mine, with two exceptions: he had a mother and a grandfather. His father left home, leaving eight children to be raised by his mother. While raising the family in a three-room shack, his mother poured out her love on him and instilled in him a love for work. They were sharecroppers, which meant that half of their small crop had to be divided with their landowners. They were poor, very poor. But while his mother gave him a certainty of love and his grandfather became a stabilizing force by setting boundaries for discipline, Dolphus still needed the fatherly approval he found in the coach who encouraged him to play college basketball.

These experiences, plus the sight of his mother locked in jail on false charges and the experience of Mississippi's closed society—these challenged him to become a man. Leaving Mississippi was his dream. However, when challenged by God to give his life in service to the folks back home, he said, "Yes, Lord, I'll return." As a result, God has used him and is using him. Dolphus has helped many to know Jesus Christ and to break out of the poverty cycle Dolphus knew so well as a child.

This book can show the ghettos of today what they need if they are going to develop leaders like Dolphus Weary. His life is a testimony. It is a challenge both to what is needed and to what will work in the inner cities of our nation and around the world. Our society has failed to develop principles that lead to indigenous leadership development, which in turn would produce leaders who will return to their neighborhoods and become the catalysts for Christian community development.

Dolphus's life story depicts a struggle. And it is evidence that the three R's of Christian community development—Relocation, Reconciliation, and Redistribution—will work.

After reading this book, no one could be unconcerned about developing indigenous leaders at the grassroots level.

Well done, my son, my brother!

PREFACE

The dream of any poor person—no matter where he grows up in the world, no matter what color his skin is—is to run as far away from poverty as he possibly can. Sometimes he ignores the voice of God in the process. I'm so thankful and glad that God didn't allow me to ignore His voice, but instead gave me the privilege to return to the poor, rural, racially torn community of Mendenhall, Mississippi, and the faith to believe that He could use me there. It's been a joy to have been a part, along with so many other people, of bringing into being Mendenhall Ministries as it is today and as God wants it to be in the future.

Since 1978, many of my friends have said to me, "Dolphus, you need to write a book about Mendenhall Ministries and your life story." For a long time, though, I rebelled against that idea because people wanted to draw attention to our work in Mendenhall. I felt we weren't ready. You see, during that year a critical decision had been made to spin off our organization from Voice of Calvary, a ministry that John Perkins had originally started in Mississippi. From then on, Mendenhall Ministries began to operate as an independent organization.

That thrust me into a new role as the one to do fund-raising, traveling, and speaking in order to generate awareness of our ministry. As I travelled around the country, I realized that we needed something to place in the hands of people that would tell about our work. But I felt that a book wasn't necessary. Not enough people know the name Dolphus Weary or Mendenhall Ministries, I reasoned, and besides, who would want to purchase a book to read about what has happened here?

In time, though, I became convinced—or convicted—that a book was right for us, as I watched God bring people who began working on it. Finally, over a period of at least two years, and through several phases, Bill Hendricks and I talked about what that book should be, and when we were ready, we actually began to work on a manuscript. So this book has been many years in the making—and I'm glad it's done!

One group of readers for whom this story is especially written are those in the Christian community who may be struggling with the thought of going back into an oppressed, impoverished community—maybe the one in which they grew up—in order to work at meeting needs there. The problem is, they don't really want to go back. If you are such a reader, I want to say that I know the struggle of going back home. I know the difficulty with identifying with the oppressed. I know the inner battle of choosing to relate fully with poor people. I know how hard it is even to think about voluntarily giving up other possibilities in order to obey God's voice.

You see, that's what this story is about—my life and my struggle with these same feelings. But it's also about God, who planned my life and brought special individuals into it in order to make me a part of His plan—a part of the wonderful thing He is doing in Simpson County, Mississippi.

O N E

"I AIN'T NEVER

COMIN' BACK!"

Dropping my basketball gear on the floor, I collapsed on the nearest bunk. My whole body ached with weariness. A tender rib especially reminded me of the elbow I'd caught on my way down from the hoop during our third game that day.

I massaged the sore spot and listened to the snores of my teammates. I longed to drop off as well. But my mind swirled with scenes from our trip.

I was midway through a six-week tour of Asia with the Crusaders, a basketball team sponsored by Overseas Crusades, a mission organization. Our group used the novelty of our height and the excitement of basketball to attract scores of Orientals to watch us play and hear our evangelistic testimonials at halftime.

Wherever we played—whether indoors in gymnasiums or outdoors on courts of asphalt, concrete, or mud, against local teams of amateurs or national teams with real talent, in tiny villages in the Philippines or big cities on Taiwan—we "tall Americans" had been well received.

I recalled the comments of some students in Hong Kong. Their teacher had asked them to practice their English by writing down their reactions to our team's appearance at their school. The results were interesting:

"The players are young, smart, and energetic. Smile is easily found from their faces."

"They sing and talk in a very funny way that make people happy and easily accept."

"Our team got a hard time in trying to beat the Crusaders because most of them are unusually tall."

"Every member are full of smile, peace, and joy."

"They preach in a different style from what we usually have listened."

One boy's comment meant more to me than all the others:

"I appreciate Mr. Weary's behavior. It is in fact a very clever device to let a Negro to be master of ceremonies, especially in Hong Kong. You know, Chinese and every people have a greater interest in things that they are short in contact with, and a Negro being with us is surely a rare sight. I am positively sure that this Mr. Weary is the most popular fellow being this morning!"

Those words played over and over in my mind. Though I'd faced dozens of teams since reading them and heard countless other endearing comments from our fans, I couldn't get over what he'd said. "Mr. Weary is the most popular fellow being this morning!"

For one of the first times in my life, I felt proud! Not just as an athletic performer, not just as a popular speaker, not even as a spokesperson for Christianity, but as a black person from America. I'd grown up in rural Simpson County, Mississippi, in the 1950s and 1960s, times of extreme racial segregation. In my boyhood I'd been cursed for my blackness, cheated and lied to because of it, locked out of the system because of it, sometimes treated like a second-class citizen.

But here in Asia in 1970, blackness was my ace-in-the-hole. The people in these countries really identified with me, especially the ones who had seen oppression themselves. In fact, my blackness really became a gift to the team and to our efforts at winning a hearing for the gospel.

I was not the tallest of the ten guys on our squad. At five-foot-eleven I was actually one of the shortest. (The only guy shorter was five-foot-six!) But I was the only black. And I think it was that, plus a certain ability to reach out to people with my personality, that made me into a sort of pied piper among our group.

We'd go into different villages where some of the people, especially the kids, had never seen a Westerner. Somehow they seemed to respond to me. They'd crowd around just to see me—and to watch and listen. Of course, it didn't hurt that I could jump higher than almost anyone else on the team. They loved that, this fellow who was shorter than the rest—just like they were shorter than we were—yet able to leap into the air and dunk the ball!

I felt a kinship with the barefoot boys who always seemed to appear at the edge of the crowds. In their secondhand clothes they reminded me of myself, running through the cotton fields not so many years back. The women washing clothes in large kettles resembled my mother, scrubbing load after load of laundry by hand for whites. The ragged boy hauling water was a picture of my brother Melvin, heading down to the cold spring that bubbled up in the woods behind our house. And the little girls toting hungry babies brought to mind my sisters.

I guess our coach, Norm Cook, recognized this bond between me and our fans, and he realized he could use it to our advantage. Whenever he could he'd get me up in front of the crowds to tell my story.

I'd been so excited to be up there in front of all those smiling, curious faces. In fact, I'd had to learn to rein in my enthusiasm. I remember one of the first times I spoke. I had to use an interpreter. I started off and just went on and on and on. Suddenly I felt the guy pulling at my coat. "Wait! Wait! Wait!" he said. "Give me a chance to tell the people what you're saying!" I'd never used an interpreter before, so I had to learn to slow down, give just a sentence or two, and then let him talk. That felt strange. But it was just one of dozens of strange, special things I'd learned on the trip.

Perhaps the strangest was what Norm had just proposed to me that evening. Taking me aside, he'd surprised me with an astounding proposal. "I like the way you relate to the people of Taiwan," he said. "In fact, wherever we go here, people seem attracted to you. When you finish seminary, why don't you consider becoming a missionary with Overseas Crusades, then return to Asia?"

I didn't know how to respond. I felt stunned, but honored. I'd never even thought of such a possibility. But Norm was a

3

persuasive guy. Mid-forties, sandy hair, a strong, handsome man with piercing eyes, he was very dynamic, a real spark plug that made the team work together. He was always talking things up, always trying to encourage us in so many ways. So when he laid the idea on me of coming back to Asia, I knew he meant it and I knew he wanted it—if it seemed best to me. So we kicked the idea around until late into the night. Finally we left it this way: I would pray about his proposition and see whether God wanted it.

What Norm couldn't know was that I was already hoping that God would give me an answer before the end of the trip. That's why I couldn't get to sleep. As I lay there on the bunk, I prayed that He would show me what He wanted, right away. To be honest, I was hoping He'd tell me to come back to Asia!

Norm's idea sounded so good. But in my head it competed with a similar challenge from another strong man who had come to mean much to me—John Perkins of the Voice of Calvary ministry in my hometown of Mendenhall, Mississippi. John had been a powerful influence on me as someone working to overturn the kind of deep-seated racism that I'd grown up with in Simpson County. When I'd left Mendenhall the year before to go to college in California, he had urged me to come back after graduation. He appealed to me not to turn my back on Mississippi, where years of discrimination had left black people without quality education, decent housing, or proper health care. Moreover, though many had religion, it, too, had become part of an oppressive system that ignored the true gospel.

My heart ached as I remembered John's words and the obvious needs in my hometown. I began feeling a tug to return and help my people. But I detested the thought of going back to Mississippi. Maybe that's why my mind was working overtime, spinning out reasons why Norm's proposal made a lot of sense. Maybe Taiwan was where God wanted me, I thought. After all, wasn't I experiencing a strong kinship with the people here, as well as those in Hong Kong and the Philippines? And wasn't my blackness an advantage here, whereas in Mississippi it was nothing but a disadvantage? In these countries I was someone special. At home I was just "nigger." No one in the world could blame me for wanting to stay far away from Simpson County.

4

"Mr. Weary is the most popular fellow being this morning!"

The boy's words made me feel as though all of Asia was reaching out and hugging me. And as I finally started to doze off, my own words seemed to pound relentlessly in my brain, words from a promise I'd sworn over and over again growing up: "Someday I'm leavin' Mississippi, and I ain't never comin' back!"

T W O

THE COTTON PATCH KID

Dolfos Weary, August 7, 1946. The midwife couldn't spell very well, and she never was sure of the date. But she did a fine job helping my mother bring me into the world.

I was born in a run-down house somewhere near the one-store hamlet of Sandy Hook, Mississippi, not far from the Louisiana border.

When I was two, our family moved back to my mother's birthplace near D'Lo, about thirty miles south of Jackson. D'Lo was supposedly named in the 1920s by a railroad conductor who had always called it "that damn low spot in the road." The U.S. Post Office cleaned it up to "D'Lo."

My father believed he could make better money sharecropping in that area. But he got discouraged when his income didn't improve, so he left my mother and eight children and went back to Louisiana. He never came back, except for one brief visit.

If you had come to visit us then, you'd have traveled down old U.S. Highway 49, a two-lane road that ran from Jackson to the Gulf Coast. It linked our rural county to the larger world. After passing through the crossroads which was D'Lo, you'd have turned down a dirt road and gone a few more miles to what was called the Gum Springs community. About five hundred feet up on the side of a hill was an unpainted wood shotgun house: three rooms and a porch.

Shotgun houses were long, narrow structures, so named because it was said you could stand at the front door and shoot a shotgun shell through every room and out the back. The first room had a fireplace for heat, a bed, and maybe a rug (which lasted about a year) to cover up the cracks in the floor. There was no linoleum. Next was the kitchen, with its wood-burning stove and a four-legged black iron dinner pot. The third room was where we lived and slept—the whole family.

Usually we had only one bed and maybe a mattress on the floor. Sleeping next to each other probably helped us survive the winter when the icy air slipped through all the cracks— cracks we tried to stuff with rags and such to keep out the drafts. In that third room we also had one chair and one dresser. There were no closets, so we hung our clothes on nails.

We had no running water or plumbing. That meant lots of trips to a spring about a half mile through the woods. A few yards from the shack was an outhouse.

Such was home for me; my mother, Lucille; and my seven brothers and sisters. Mama called us her "stairsteps." Charles and Joe Louis, my half brothers, were the oldest. Charles eventually went to school and became an electrician. He used his income to buy us lots of little things that Mama could never afford. Joe Louis left Mississippi in the early 1950s, like so many blacks, and moved to New York City. He developed diabetes and died when he was only twenty-two.

In my immediate family the oldest was Albert, who also left for New York. Then came Elgie. Whenever we all worked together in the fields picking cotton or corn, Elgie and I always seemed to end up dreaming about the future, about our hopes for a better life. She was the first in the family to go to college, so she served as a model for me and the others.

My brother Melvin, though, was the genius among us. A straight-*A* student, he was a wizard at mechanical and electrical things. He eventually built a house for Mama, and later he moved to D.C. to run his own cab business.

I came next, followed by Katharine and Patricia. Katharine was like Elgie and me, always dreaming about a better life. Eventually she got it, making her way to Grand Rapids to work in curriculum development for the school system there. Patricia was a real inspiration to me. She married right out of high school and had two children. When they were older, she determined to get her college degree, even though it meant attending a night school sixty miles away. Finally she graduated, and she is now a teacher.

Mama eventually remarried to a farmer named Bill Craft and had two more children, Virgie Bell and Billy.

I have warm memories of my family, but it was a constant struggle for us just to survive. We had no steady source of income. Mama did whatever she could to earn money. She washed clothes for white people—two loads a day for fifty or seventy-five cents a load. She scrubbed their floors. She cleaned eggs at a poultry house up the road when the work was available. And of course she farmed. Her father lived across the road, and our house was surrounded by his four acres of cotton and five acres of corn.

Picking cotton became a way of life for us, as it did for so many blacks in the South. Mama picked cotton and taught each of us how to pick it by the time we were ten. I suppose some people might view the image of blacks out in the cotton fields as part of the charm of a culture that has passed away. But it was anything but charming if you were one of the "niggers" in the fields!

Cotton picking season began in late August and ended right before Thanksgiving. Sometimes we'd get out to the fields as early as four in the morning, partly to beat the heat, but partly, too, because the dew made the cotton heavier, which brought us more income when it was weighed.

Once we got Grandpa's cotton picked, we went to work for white folks who came in trucks to take us to their fields. They paid us two and a half cents a pound. My brother Melvin boasted that he could pick 400 pounds a day. But I doubted it. Three hundred pounds would be an incredible day.

One morning I picked 175 pounds before we stopped for lunch. I was sure I was on my way to more than 300 pounds. But in my enthusiasm I ate so much and drank so much cold water that I was laid out sick most of the afternoon. I probably only got another 30 or 40 pounds in.

On a good day you could pick 200 pounds. In a pretty good year you could get 2,000 pounds of cotton from an acre. But in a terrible year you'd only get a bale out of every four or five acres. Then you'd be in real trouble financially, plus you'd feel awful about all the work you'd put in, just to get a small return.

And it was a *lot* of work, especially for kids just ten or eleven years old. There were no child labor laws protecting us. People just figured that since we were black and poor, anything was OK. Neither did anybody (except Mama) worry about how many days we missed school because it was natural. It was expected. It was the way things were. School for the white kids started around the first to the middle of September. But for us, school started around the last of October or the first part of November.

Not that it took that long to pick the cotton, but most kids stayed out of school to harvest the corn as well. Corn could stay in the fields a lot longer than cotton, which lost value as it dried out. So the corn was left for last, and the kids who picked it didn't get to school until around Thanksgiving.

In addition to cotton and corn, we had other produce to gather in as well. After Mama picked up the sweet potatoes, for instance, we put them in sacks and hauled them to banks in the garden and covered them with pine needles. This became part of our winter food supply.

Daily chores included getting oak for the fireplace and pine kindling for the stove. We'd stack it all on the porch so that when it rained or was cold we could just open the door and get a log for the fire.

After supper each night we did our schoolwork with a kerosene lamp providing the light. Even though we missed a lot of school, and even though our schools lacked a lot that the white schools had, and even though my mother had little education herself, she believed strongly in education. I think it had to do with her own background. She'd dropped out of school in tenth grade. All of her teachers were against it because she was so smart, and they figured she had what it took to go to college. But she'd had enough of farming and things at home, and a fellow promised the moon if she'd drop out and marry him. She did.

10

It was a mistake. The marriage turned bad, and she was left with kids and no marketable skills. So I think that she wanted to make sure that each of her children would have the opportunities she'd never had. She wanted every one of us to finish high school and tried to help each of her daughters to be able to go to college. She felt we boys should be able to make it on our own, but she would do anything she could to help us.

That's why she always let the white man know after we got through picking cotton that no child of hers was going to stay home from school to gather corn, too. Instead, she herself would break the ears off while we went to school. Then we'd pick them up later and load them into a crib.

I remember that one spring a man asked her if I could put out fertilizer for him. She told him, "Well, I guess he can today, but no more after that, even if I have to get out there and do it myself. When you keep them out of school even one day, there's something they miss."

People got to where they'd say, "Oh, Lucille is education crazy." It wasn't until I was grown-up and saw the big picture of segregation that I understood what a courageous thing my mother was doing. Most of the white landowners had no interest in seeing a black person get an education. Education meant freedom for the blacks. But it meant that the white man would lose his source of cheap labor. Furthermore, it meant that he couldn't treat black folk as dumb niggers and cheat them out of money and such.

But education meant everything to Mama. She believed in her children going to school, and she always worked to see that we stayed in school. She didn't want us to have to go through life the way she had, struggling to get by. It amazed me the way she managed, despite her own lack of education. Every morning Mama mixed and rolled out dough for thirty-two biscuits. She didn't have meat, but she had syrup and butter, and "poor man's gravy" made from lard, flour, and water. At Christmas time, though, we ate in style—a hen or a rooster with dumplings and dressing. To top it off she'd bake four cakes—chocolate, jelly, plain, and coconut—and maybe even an egg custard pie. All of this was very special because we couldn't afford it from day-to-day. Our Christmas presents would be two apples and two oranges each, plus a little candy. The boys usually got packets of firecrackers—simple treats, obviously, but we thought they were really something!

During most of the rest of the year our food consisted of flour to make biscuits, flour to make gravy, and sugar for syrup. It wasn't until I went to college that I learned that breakfast for many white folks often included eggs, toast, jelly, milk, orange juice, and bacon. Having food like that on a regular basis was unimaginable to us. A few black families fared a little better if they had a father in the house to raise a hog or a cow for meat and milk. Somehow, on her own, my Mama did the best she could and kept the family together and alive.

One winter was worse than usual. I think it was 1962. It had snowed, which was rare for Mississippi, and a bitter cold wind kept all of us by the stove all day. When dinnertime came, we had no food. The closest little store was three miles away. Since there was no one with a car to drive us, Melvin started on foot without boots or gloves. Mama and the rest of us huddled by the stove, listening to the wind. We knew that Melvin would have to face into it on his way back, so we started worrying about him. When he finally returned, his hands were literally frozen to the grocery sack. We had to peel away the paper.

In bed that night, lying next to him, I knew he was suffering. He didn't sleep—his hands ached too badly. I hurt inside to see my brother suffer just so we could have a little food. I'll never forget his courage.

Melvin wasn't the only one of us trying to help Mama out. I remember when we first got electricity. I was eight years old. My older brother Charlie had gone to a nearby vocational school for blacks, where he took an interest in electrical work. He ran a wire from our house to an electrical pole not too far away. Then he hung a light bulb by the door. That was such a big deal for us, but since we weren't paying for it, Mama made him take it down. She was like that—always honest, even when it cost her. Several years later Charles *legally* wired our house.

My first trip to a doctor was for a stomachache that wouldn't go away. The doctor diagnosed it as worms. Who knows whether or not I really had worms—lots of kids were said to have worms. His medicine didn't work, though. My stomachache wasn't cured. So Mama put together one of her home remedies—a teaspoon of sugar with a drop or two of turpentine. It worked! In fact, there weren't many sicknesses she couldn't cure one way or another. For colds she'd give us castor oil! As if that weren't bad enough, she'd add a drop of turpentine to that, too.

I guess poor people are the masters at home remedies. They can't afford regular treatment, so they find something else—perhaps corn-shuck tea, an awful-tasting brew made by boiling shucks of corn. Or maybe they go out and find some branches or some roots and make root tea. Today when somebody gets cut, we rush them to the doctor. But I remember how we'd pull spider webs out of all the corners of the house and put them on the cut place. That really helped stop the bleeding and heal up the wound. Whatever the cure was, it was something that people had used time out of mind, and it often worked. One of our greatest pleasures was the rolling store. The rolling store was like a step van or panel truck that carried the kinds of things you find in convenience stores nowadays. Since we lived so far from any stores, and because not many people in the area had pickup trucks or cars, the rolling store made its rounds on the back roads of the county. The driver sounded his horn a mile away to announce his coming. By the time he arrived, crowds of barefoot children would be waiting, clutching pennies and eager to buy potato chips, cookies, candy bars, and white bread, or as we called it, "light bread."

The most popular item was stageplank, a thin gingerbread-type of cake with pink icing, about eight inches long and four inches wide. At two for a nickel, this was the best buy because ten or twelve children could share a package of two. They still sell stageplank today—at about half the size and three times the cost!

To be honest, I don't know if I even liked stageplank much. But when you grow up in poverty and are always having to do without, when it finally comes time to buy a treat, taste really has nothing to do with it. What matters is that it's the biggest! Poor folk always want the biggest. Bigger means better. The biggest is the best. It'll last! That was our value system.

Somehow along the way we ended up with a black-and-white television set. That really opened up a whole new world for me—a world that seemed unreal. I remember watching cartoons and the commercials, and there were two things I started dreaming about having—ice cream and a choice of cereal. Very simple things, really. But unknown in our house.

I was probably ten or eleven before I tasted my first ice cream. We went to town and went into a store that had Eskimo pies. I thought it was the best stuff you could eat, all that vanilla ice cream covered in chocolate and packaged in a silver wrapper. (Later on I discovered cones.) We thought ice cream was the best because we had it so rarely. We had no refrigerator, so I dreamed about someday having one and being able to open it up and see ice cream.

And cereal, too! I always thought how great it would be to be able to pick and choose between Kellogg's Corn Flakes and Cheerios. We never had cereal. We never could afford it.

When you grow up like that, you don't dread not having things—you dream about having them. Even the simplest things feel like luxuries. Even today I tell my wife, Rosie, that the most exciting part of our home is the bathroom—to be able to go in there and fill up the tub with water. She gets on me: "How come you put so much water in the tub?!" But for nineteen years my family never had a bathroom with running water or a toilet.

The first time I ever got to take a real shower was in college. Believe it or not, I had to figure out how to use the plumbing! *What is this strange thing?* I wondered. Something as simple as a hot shower or sitting relaxed in a tub of water—it's a fantastic luxury when you grow up without it but know it's possible.

You might think that all of this yearning would have made me squander what little money I was given on stageplank and ice cream. I didn't. I was the saver in the family. One time when Mama gave me a quarter for lunch money, I didn't eat a thing all day. I knew we were having baked potatoes and collard greens that night for supper, so I figured I could make it till then and saved my quarter. I'm still like that.

We lived at a survival level, but there was one important way in which we were very, very rich: we had the strength of our home. It was really the strength of my mother, the historical strength of the black woman—a woman facing insurmountable odds, yet a woman who dared to say, "I'm going to raise my children with a sense of morality, with a sense of honesty, and with a sense of, 'If you're going to get it, you're going to have to work hard for it. Nobody's going to give it to you.'"

You could see that kind of determination in the way Mama worked and in her value on education. You could also see it in the way she raised us kids. She didn't miss a trick!

I remember one time when my sister Elgie was seventeen, she was paid a visit by a young man. Mama had told her, "Don't you be goin' out on that front porch with the light off!" Well, it got late, and the fellow had to go. Elgie saw him to the door, and he went out on the porch. The light was off. Elgie didn't go out with him, but she stood with her head leaning out the front door—sort of obeying Mama's rule and sort of bending it, too! All of a sudden Mama came up quietly behind her and whapped the door open with a bang! She yanked her daughter back inside, slapped her, and said, "Git yerself back in here! You know what I tole you!" The boy came back in and started to apologize, but no apology was needed. "She know she not s'posed to be out there with the light off!" Mama told him. The way she saw it, it was Elgie's responsibility to do right—not the young man's. It didn't matter that Elgie only had her head out the door—that was too much! I know Elgie was as embarrassed as any seventeen-year-old could be in a situation like that. But she respected her Mama. She had reason to.

Mama was a strong woman with strong character. And she passed that on to her children. I know for me it showed in the way I became the peacemaker in the lot. When my brothers and sisters would fight, I didn't like it. Even though they were older, I'd try to get in between them and break up the argument or scuffle. Sometimes they'd take me by the collar and shove me aside. But Mama said I was "kind of grown-up in the head," meaning I had a sense of adult responsibility about me. If something had to be done and everyone was arguing about it, I'd step in and say, "Look, it's got to be done! Mama says it's got to be done. So why aren't we doing it? It's OK for us to disagree, but we've got to get it done!"

Every one of us kids became something because of Mama. The luxury that Dolphus Weary and his brothers and sisters had was a strong mother who encouraged us to become the best we could be.

She had some help in that from her father. Even though Grandpa didn't live in our house, he was a strong male figure who provided discipline that we understood. In many ways he became the father we never had. Like Mama, he inspired us to do our best. He believed in using time and money wisely and not being wasteful. And when he told us to do something, he expected to be obeyed. One day in the cotton field I found out the hard way.

"Dolphus, use both hands to pick the cotton!" he shouted to me. When you pick cotton you can pick a lot more if you use two hands. You move a lot faster. But often I'd get to daydreaming and wishing I was someplace else. Then I'd slow down and rest my back by leaning my elbow on my knee, picking with just one hand. I wouldn't get much done that way!

Well, that's what he was yelling about. So I perked up and used both hands. But after a while, I slipped back to one. Again he ordered: "Dolphus, both hands!" Instantly I picked up the pace, using both hands. But somehow I slacked off again. That time, he came over and grabbed hold of me. I could tell he was angry. He grabbed a cotton stalk and started whipping me.

"Dolphus, I've told you three times!" he shouted. Down came that stalk as he thrashed me on my legs, not once but many times. He was a strong man, and it stung.

I was kicking and shouting. "Stop, Grandpa! I'll . . . do . . . it . . . right!" I could hardly get the words out, it hurt so bad. Mama had to grease me when I got home.

But Grandpa wasn't all sternness. I remember another time when he felt better about my work. He was fussy—he liked to have his cotton hoed three times. When you plant cotton, you plant the seeds extremely close together. When it comes up, the plants are only about an inch apart. To grow properly, they need to be thinned to six or eight inches apart. So you go in and "chop cotton," that is hoe out a lot of the plants, plus any grass that's come up. Later, when the cotton is about six or eight inches high, you go back and hoe out the grass again. We had no herbicides. So to keep the grass down we had to hoe it a second time.

We could have left it at that. But Grandpa was such a perfectionist that he wanted his cotton hoed a third time, to be clean, without any grass. That was how he took care of his fields, his home, everything. It all had to be just right.

So one day he wanted my brothers and me to hoe his cotton a third time. We refused. But the next morning I decided to help him after all. Years later Mama told me that he never forgot that I did that. I never forgot it either. He was trying to teach me that I really ought to do a good job the *first* time around.

Grandpa was such an encourager to me. Chopping cotton in the fields with him, I'd talk about my dreams and what I wanted to do when I was grown-up.

"Doc"—that's what he always called me—"you're going to be a doctor someday." He'd say that again and again.

"Me? A country boy?"

He felt sure it would happen.

One day I remember telling him, "Grandpa, I want to finish school and help people, teach people."

"Doc, you keep on doing things right and you will! You will, boy." Little did I realize how wise he was.

T H R E E

THE RELIGION OF

SHACKS AND CADILLACS

If there was one ray of hope for us in an otherwise hopeless situation, it was religion. Sunday became the one day in the week when we could leave behind the cotton fields, our ramshackle house, and the white man, and instead look forward to a better life to come. Church was the place where we could celebrate our unique culture.

The day began with our biggest meal of the week. We'd get up, and Mama would have salmon patties going. She'd buy a nineteen-cent can of salmon and mix it with flour and so forth until it became like a hash. Then she'd press it into patties and fry it. It seemed like a special meal at the time, but maybe it's why I can't stand seafood today!

Occasionally we'd have a chicken. I couldn't believe that one chicken could be cut into ten pieces! Everybody would get a little piece, but we'd fight over who got the breast—not because it was the best, but because it was the biggest. Mama would also make up some biscuits and gravy, and sometimes some rice. That was our big meal of the week.

Then we'd dress up for church. I say "dress up"—as if we had special clothing! Actually, my Sunday best was usually a pair of jeans and a white shirt, or a shirt that was a little different than what I'd wear every other day. My whole wardrobe then was

19

never more than a pair of khaki pants, two pairs of jeans, and maybe three shirts.

Rain or shine, we all walked three miles down the road to the Shiloh Baptist Church. It was a typical wood-framed, white church building with movable wooden benches that could seat about two hundred. Off to one side of the property was a cemetery.

Mama was extremely diligent to get us there every Sunday by nine-thirty for Sunday school. There were no classrooms, just the big sanctuary, so all the classes huddled in different corners and had their lessons, something that still happens in many churches.

Sunday school lasted until noon. That was because a lot of people took turns commenting on the lessons. This went on and on. Some of the people would just repeat what others said, and some just got up because if there was a silent moment, they felt they ought to say something.

Later I realized how important this opportunity to speak was. Aside from church, there was no other formal setting for a black person to express himself as a human being. There was no place for him to sing his songs, except in the fields. There was no place for him to make a speech, to give an opinion, or to exercise leadership. Church gave him a lot of dignity, a place where he mattered.

Once a month we'd have a Pastoral Sunday. Most pastors, like ours, served a number of churches, visiting each church one Sunday a month. When our pastor came, it was a big deal. After a break from Sunday school, we all came back for the main service. We'd sing songs that had an emotional, nostalgic feel to them.

Then the preacher would get up and start preaching. His message was designed to stir up the emotions of the people. His words, his tone, his whole demeanor played on their feelings. A favorite ploy was to get them worked up over the loss of a loved one. "Remember how your mother used to hug you?" he'd ask. "Remember how she loved you? You was her baby! But she no longer here now, is she? You want to see her, don't you? But she gone! She in that grave out there! She can't come tuck you into bed no more!" And people would be sniffing and sobbing. He'd keep reminding them of their mothers until they were in a frenzy. Then he'd shout, "But someday you goin' to see her again! Someday you be goin' to heaven, and there she'll be—with her arms wide open, waitin' for you! How many of you can see her standin' there? How many of you can't wait for that day?"

Sooner or later somebody would let go and start shouting, speaking in tongues, twitching, trembling, or even fainting. Ushers rushed to catch them and cool them with hand-held fans until they regained consciousness.

In describing all this, I'm not saying that people didn't respond legitimately. Looking back, I believe that many were really moved by the Spirit. Nevertheless, the goal of the preacher was this: getting someone to shout.

It was all great entertainment, led by the one figure in the black community who was allowed to be successful. We never saw a black doctor or a black lawyer or any other black professional. No one of our race had any status in the larger community.

So what we didn't have we transferred to our preacher. We gave him as much as we could of the best that we had. I remember him coming out to our house for dinner. He'd drive up in a big, shiny Cadillac, and he'd be wearing a new suit. And my mother would have worked and sweated extra hard to get enough money together to buy an extra chicken and such to feed him and his guests.

While they feasted, we kids would sit around and watch them, waiting to see what would be left for us. I came to resent it, but Mama took real joy in it because the payoff for her was that the preacher would recognize her later in a sermon. During a week of revival meetings, for instance, he'd stand up and say, "Sister Lucille really cooked! She made the best chicken and the best pie! I mean she had the table spread, and it was really good!"

Then all the other ladies who had to cook for him the other nights would get stirred up, thinking how they were going to have to fix more and do more. It was a competition to see who could please the preacher most.

You could see this reflected in the collections. In our church we took up two collections—one for the poor and one for the preacher. The one for the poor was taken before the sermon. It may sound strange to hear about people who had as little as we had collecting money for the poor. But it was a real attempt to teach us that no matter how little you have, you still have a responsibility toward someone somewhere—in the church or in the community—who has less than you have.

After the sermon we took up another collection, the one for the preacher. We were expected to give to both. It used to bother me, though, when I'd see people drop nickels and dimes into the poor offering and hold onto their dollars to drop into the offering for the preacher. I'd sit there and think, *I'd like to see somebody turn this thing around!*

That second offering would last up to half an hour. The ushers would guide us one-by-one to a table in the front where three or four people would be counting the money. There would be music and singing all the while; it was a real ritual.

Some people could afford to put in a dollar bill. They'd take out that dollar and almost wave it to let everyone see—including the preacher, of course. We even had a few ladies who waited until everyone else had gone around. It was funny how they'd deliberately hold back until everybody else was seated. Then they'd get up and hold that dollar so everyone could see it.

Another ritual connected with that second offering was setting a goal for a certain amount of money. If the deacons didn't collect enough the first time, they'd take up the offering again. If they still didn't get it, they'd say, "We'd like twenty-five dollars. Who's going to give some money for this?" Since people loved recognition, somebody in the back would jump up: "I've got a dollar! Here's a dollar!" Soon they'd have twenty-eight dollars. Then they'd say, "OK, we've got twenty-eight now. If we just had two more, we could make thirty!" And some more people would give.

Some deacons got so good at making appeals that they became "professionals" at it. Often they would visit other churches, and the leaders there would recruit them to handle collection duties because they knew the visiting deacons could get the offering.

Every first Sunday of the month we were assessed church dues. Someone would write your name down and collect your dues—usually a dollar or two for an adult man, a dollar for a woman, and twenty-five cents for each child. Then they took time to read off who paid what. In that way we raised the budget for the church.

No one could ever tell just how big the membership was at our church. On a Pastoral Sunday the sanctuary might be three-quarters full, but a lot of those folks were from other churches. The next Sunday they'd be at a different church, along with a lot of our regulars.

The biggest church event of the year was the revival, a week of eating, singing, preaching, and fund-raising. The church was scrubbed from top to bottom, the graveyard, usually overgrown with weeds and grass, was cleaned up. Relatives from as far away as Detroit and Chicago would plan their vacations around revival week. So you'd see license plates from all over.

It all began with Revival Sunday. We'd have Sunday school and a worship service that ended around one-thirty or two. Then we'd stop for a time we called "dinner on the grounds." Ladies in the church fixed boxes of food that included fried chicken and dressing and cakes and pies and such. We'd go around to different boxes and fill up our plates. Then we'd eat, sitting on the tailgates of cars and trucks or on the ground under the trees.

After that they'd get people back inside for the evening service, which started around four or four-thirty. This was the time for our choir to sing its special numbers. The choir practiced for weeks in preparation. They sang soul-stirring hymns as well as songs from slavery times. Naturally they sang such spirituals as "Steal Away" and "Swing Low, Sweet Chariot." Most of the songs pointed to the hereafter rather than the reality of living now: "In the Sweet Bye and Bye," "I'll Fly Away," "Just Over in Glory Land." They talked about "one day," about how "farther along" we'll understand. Life is a struggle now, but someday we'll understand why.

I recall one song in particular that went:

> I do not know why all around me
> My hopes all shattered seem to be.
> But God's perfect plan I cannot see.
> But one day, someday, He'll make it plain.

I cannot tell the depth of love
That moves the Father's heart above.
My test is something my love to prove,
But someday I'll understand.

I don't understand my struggles now,
Why I suffer, and feel so bad.
But one day, someday, He'll make it plain.

Someday when I His face shall see,
Someday from tears I shall be free,
Yes, someday I'll understand.

You can see the psychology at work here: I don't have to deal with my poverty, my troubles. Someday when I get to heaven I'll understand it all. A song like "I've Got Shoes" meant that all of God's children are supposed to have shoes. I may not have mine now, but one day, when I get to heaven, I will. Then I'll walk all over heaven! That assurance would mean a lot to somebody who didn't have shoes. It would give him a tremendous sense of hope.

Of course, the preachers got to enjoy their hopes a lot sooner than the rest of us, thanks to the offerings collected during Revival Week. A poor community like Gum Springs left a thousand dollars or more in the offering plate by the time it was all over. The evangelist would take most of the money home with him to Jackson or wherever he lived, and our community saw very little of it. Somehow that didn't seem to matter to us. We were proud to do whatever it took to satisfy our preacher. By making him successful, we transformed our own inadequacies and failures into an image of success. Watching him depart in his Cadillac, knowing he had the best we could provide, made us feel good. He was our only picture of a black person enjoying power and prosperity.

This was the religion I grew up with. It was a system that entertained more than it instructed. It was designed to make us feel good, or at least to feel *something*, rather than to change our character. It measured its success by how much money was raised and how well the preacher lived, not by whether people responded to the gospel, or whether the needs of the poor were met. Justice issues were never really discussed, and the hope offered was completely other-worldly.

Nevertheless, somewhere along the way I heard a call to make some kind of personal commitment to God. I was seven years old, attending a revival meeting. At the end of the sermon, the preacher invited folks to join the church. I watched people around me, young and old, make their way down the front, shake the preacher's hand, and add their names to the church roll. I looked up at Mama and asked, "Can I join the church?"

"No, you're too young yet," she said. "Wait a little."

All year I waited. The next year at revival time I asked again: "Can I join the church?" This time she nodded her head, so I walked down the aisle and I shook the preacher's hand. I heard him say, "Now you're a member of the church. After you're baptized, you'll be an official member of the church."

The church had no baptistery, so we gathered at a pond owned by a member of the church. Before the baptism started, somebody tapped on the surface and got some ripples going to run the snakes out. Then those of us who were to be baptized waded in and the preacher baptized us. I became a part of the religious system.

The church leaders then told me what the conditions were for being a Christian: "Dolphus, if you keep coming to church . . . if you go to Sunday school . . . if you join the choir . . . if you become a junior deacon or Sunday school teacher . . ."

I believed that if I did all these kinds of things, God would take me to heaven when I died. I was never told anything about having a personal relationship with God. I just responded to the religion that was offered me. So I worked hard at being good, trying again and again to do all that was required. The words of a song we learned in choir became my theme:

> I'm working,
> Trying to make a hundred,
> Ninety-nine and a half won't do.

I had to be perfect! God expected 100-percent perfection. He'd turn me away if I fell short even a little bit. But the more I thought about it, the more I felt afraid.

One day a lady came to our school and handed out little packets of Bible verses. "Whoever memorizes these verses can earn a free trip to camp," she told us. That was all I needed to hear! I learned the verses in no time at all, and soon I was on my way to Camp Pioneer near Jackson.

On the first night we all sat around a campfire. It was a special moment. I liked being there, away from the poverty of Gum Springs. I also liked the friends I was already making at camp. We felt close as we joined together in campfire songs. Then someone got up and talked about giving your life to Jesus. I didn't really understand it all, but it seemed to speak to the fear I'd felt about this religion in general. So, when an invitation to "accept Christ" was offered, I bowed my head and prayed the prayer that the leader gave us. Whatever else happened, I felt closer to God. Surrounded by friends, I could wholeheartedly join in singing: "My Lord knows the way through the wilderness!"

Two weeks later I was home again, only I had no one to teach me or encourage me in spiritual matters. I was back in the old system that stressed working your way to heaven. So I pushed myself to greater efforts: I never missed a Sunday, I helped the pastor and other church leaders, and I studied my Sunday school lessons. Still, the words of the song kept coming back to haunt me: "Ninety-nine and a half won't do." What if I fail? What if I don't make a hundred? I was confused. I was scared. And I was miserable.

Revival time came around again. As usual, the pastor concluded the service by asking everybody to bow their heads. "All of you who know you're not a Christian, raise your hand." I felt that because I hadn't made it to perfection yet, I wasn't a Christian. So I raised my hand. Then the preacher said, "Those of you who raised your hands, come and join the church."

Well, that really confused me! I was already a member of the church! In my heart I knew I was a sinner. But I couldn't go up and join the church again! My fears just multiplied. I didn't know what to do. I remember going home and crying and crying. "What's wrong?" Mama asked me. But I couldn't explain what I felt inside me, the hopelessness and anguish. All I could do was sob, "I just can't do it! I just can't do it!"

Time passed, and I tried to forget my pain and my failure as a religious person. I relaxed a little. *Maybe I'm OK,* I thought. *After all, I'm no worse than the next person, and I'm sure a lot better than some!* I was fifteen, and I didn't smoke and didn't drink. I was not engaged in what was called "riotous living." I was basically a good sinner.

And I still attended church. But I began to rebel against the system. I watched the preachers come and go, draining the meager financial resources of our people, unconcerned with the conditions we lived in. It seemed like all they cared about was how well we took care of them. They'd even mention other churches and their pastors in their sermons: "They lo-o-ove their pastor!" meaning that that church had just raised enough money to send the man on a trip.

It was bad enough when the whites took advantage of us. But it seemed to me that the black preachers exploited us a lot, too. And they got away with it because we didn't think enough of ourselves to challenge the system. We were a defeated people, without spirit and without expectations for anything better. At least not in the South.

F O U R

LABOR

AND LYNCHINGS

Beginning in 1915 and continuing through the post-war years, more than 2 million black people left the Deep South. They headed for the big cities in the North, cities like Cleveland, Chicago, Detroit, and New York, or to California. Every family had its own reasons for getting out. But I believe most of them felt the way I came to feel: *No matter what I do, no matter how hard I work, I'll always be second-class here. The system is rigged against me, and I'll always make just enough to get by, but never enough to get ahead. That's the way it is here, and it's never going to change!*

Farming was a good example. We farmed Grandpa's ten acres with only a mule and hand tools. We used insecticides to some degree, but really never had the training to know all the ones that were available, nor how to use them effectively. Even if we had, we never had much money to invest in chemicals. So whatever yield our crops gave us mostly depended on the weather and sheer hard work.

Yet we never made a real profit. In a good year an acre was supposed to yield a bale of cotton, in an exceptionally good year a bale and a half. In a bad year, when the boll weevils damaged the cotton plants, an acre might only yield half a bale or less. I remember a few years when we only got one bale from four acres. It sold for just $150—not even enough to pay back the landowner for the money we'd borrowed to buy our half of the seeds and fertilizer.

During these extra-lean times my sister Elgie and I arranged to work another piece of property two miles down the road in hopes of earning better money. But as the harvest neared, we could see that our work here was also in vain. Finally, it came time to pick what little cotton there was.

At the end of the first row, Elgie collapsed in dismay on the Mississippi soil. "We'll never get even a bale if it's all like this!" she cried. I'd never seen her look so defeated. Nothing I could say would make her feel better, either, because what she said was true. We returned to the picking, but our hearts weren't in it. It was a terrible harvest.

Down on the highway, cars kept whizzing by on their way to Jackson. Finally I stood up. "Elgie, someday we're gonna drive a car down that highway, too!" My sister stopped picking and looked at the traffic. Then she nodded, and I could tell she was as determined as I was to make it true. Then we started pointing at various makes and models as they passed, saying, "That one's mine!" It helped us lighten up and pass the time faster.

In the end, even though we'd hoed those three acres really well, the poor soil there and lack of money for fertilizer worked against us. We got almost nothing for our labor. We tried again the next year, but we didn't get even a single full bale in two years' time.

About that time a white man that my stepfather knew invited us to come to his forty or fifty acres near Magee and farm on halves. Sharecropping, or farming on halves, as it was called, meant farming on land belonging to a white man. He'd supply the seed and fertilizer and such and the blacks would supply the labor. Then when the harvest came in, half the crop went to the landowner and half to the blacks, only first their half had to repay any debts they had incurred while the crop was growing.

On the whole, our experience with sharecropping worked out OK. But for many blacks, it was a system that kept them mired in debt and poverty. Sharecropping had to be done just the way the white man said. He'd tell them how he wanted the seed planted and how he wanted the fertilizer used. It was as if the sharecropper didn't know anything about farming. Sometimes the owner would slip around to see if things were being done just the way he wanted them, and if not, he'd call the blacks ignorant or disobedient. It didn't matter whether the black person had ideas of his own or knew a better way. A black was trained not to think. If he did anything his own way, it meant he was sly or underhanded—so the whites believed.

Any improvements made on the land, such as repairing fences, benefited the owner, even though it was not his labor or supplies that were used. No allowances were made for that work. Even if the black man did things just the way the landowner wanted, if the crop was poor, he could lose all of his belongings—even his mule and tools—to pay the landowner back. If the black man's wife had put her mark on the agreement, the landlord could take all her household supplies, too. Few black people were well-educated, and they didn't know anything about the laws except what they were told.

In years when the crop was poor, a sharecropper might get into debt and have to mortgage his mule, wagon, and other gear to his boss. Later the boss might borrow money, using the sharecropper's mortgaged property as security. In this way, the black man, through ignorance or necessity, sometimes ended up paying off the white man's debts as well as his own. For a lot of black sharecroppers, life became an endless string of debts, and in the end they were left with nothing.

The white man also dominated the sharecropper through the stores. As a black person growing up, you were really a nobody. You only mattered to the extent that you were useful to a white. So when a sharecropper went to work for a white man, the white would call up a grocery store and say, "Let Dolphus shop there. He's OK." Whenever the black man shopped there, the owner would record the purchases in a book.

The only groceries we ever bought in the stores were just staples—flour and salt and such. Everything else we grew ourselves, or else we just did without. We raised hogs and slaughtered them to make lard by frying up the fat. We grew corn for corn bread. We had a few chickens running around. We didn't have utilities to pay or a mortgage or a car payment, so our expenses at the store were minimal.

Even so, we were always in a role of dependency on whites. This became a real problem during the civil rights movement.

Blacks would start pressing for change and standing up for their rights, and a white man would say, "But Jimmie, haven't I always taken care of you?" And Jimmie would be in a bind. He'd have to say, "Yessir, you're right! You always let me shop in the stores."

Perhaps the reason I avoided the worst of the sharecropping system was because I got burned by it at an early age. When I was nine, we did some sharecropping for a man who supplied the land, the tools, and the mules. We supplied the labor. He loaned us money throughout the year to buy our basic necessities. He also kept the books. The first year was a poor one for farming. At the end we were in debt $200—according to his records.

The next year, though, we produced three times as much as the first year. We figured this crop would mean some money for us. But at the end of harvesttime he told us we'd only broken even. I was outraged! We'd worked so hard! I was only nine, but I was beginning to feel trapped and hopeless.

But not totally. We children decided to keep our own records the next year. This time we had a pretty good crop. After harvesting and marketing all of it, we came to the landlord and showed him how we'd come out ahead. Reluctantly he agreed, but we could tell that our sharecropping days were numbered. We didn't wait for the landlord to order us off the property. We packed up ourselves and went back to Grandpa's farm.

When I was thirteen, my father died. Elgie, Albert, and I went to Louisiana for his funeral. Mama stayed home. When we got to Louisiana, we stayed with one of my sisters. She had very little to offer us, but she cooked up a big pot of grits. I still remember eating cold grits all that time. It was all that she had to feed us.

I didn't really know how to feel toward my dad. He'd been a nonentity in my life. Mama used to talk about the fact that he lived in Columbia, Mississippi. But with no contact, no letters, no nothing, I had no desire to know him. Nobody told me I was supposed to try and get in touch with him. With Grandpa around, we just related to him instead.

My father worked construction or something from the time I was born. So he was away all the time. He deserted the family for good when I was quite young. Once we all realized he was gone, Mama turned our energies toward living rather than toward hating him or worrying about him.

He only returned one time. There was something he wanted to arrange so that my family could start receiving his Social Security checks. He showed up, but I didn't know who he was until Mama told me, "This is your father." Later on the checks started coming. I was grateful that he did that, but even so, he was a nonentity.

So his funeral had no meaning for me. I'm not quite sure whether Elgie cried or not. Other people seemed remorseful. But I felt no sense of loss, even though he was my father, because he'd never been a part of my life to begin with.

About that same time I made a new friend named Jimmie Walker. Jimmie had attended a church school down the road that went up to sixth grade. In the seventh grade he started coming to the school in Mendenhall, which was were I met him.

I always envied Jimmie. He was a good athlete, very energetic. His aunt had lived in Chicago and worked all her life. She had moved back to Simpson County for some reason, and he lived with her. They had this big black Cadillac that he used to drive around, and I'd think, *Look at this guy driving this car! The biggest and the best!*

We became great friends. He'd come up to our place to help out with the farming, and then I'd go down to his place to help his people. We'd compete to see who could finish the work first.

One day when Jimmie and I were in the cotton fields, I asked him, "Do you ever think about going to college?"

"Yeah, but I don't know how I'd pay for it." Even though his aunt had worked hard over the years, Jimmie's family still had the same problem my family did—never enough money.

"I don't know how I would, either," I replied. "But I sure would like to go to Mississippi Valley State. College or not, though, if things don't get better around here for black folks, I'm gettin' outta this state after high school!"

As I made that daring announcement, I stopped picking cotton and looked past the rows, beyond the fields as far as my imagination could take me. I saw myself finishing college and becoming a math teacher. I'd get married and have a family and make some real money and become the kind of provider my own family had never had. I'd make something of myself. Poverty was no longer an option. And Mississippi was definitely no longer an option. I'd get out—and never come back!

But the dream quickly dissolved as we watched the new bright yellow school bus drive by, bringing the white kids home from school. I felt sick. Jimmie did, too. That bus always reminded us of how much better everything was for white people. Our bus was old and rickety. The tires were worn. The windows wouldn't stay up in winter. The seats had springs poking through. Furthermore, watching those white kids come home from school made us doubly depressed because they were able to be in school, while we had to stay out in the fields until the cotton was harvested. It seemed like no matter what area of life you looked at, the system kept us from getting ahead. Jimmie and I didn't say anything more. We knew our thoughts were the same.

After a while I blurted out something that was bothering me a lot. "Our white neighbor moved his fence fifty feet onto our property!"

"You gonna let him get away with it?"

"I don't want to. I'm angry! But Mama doesn't want us to say anything to him."

"But Dolphus, you know how much land that comes to?"

"It's three acres. I figured it out. I want to get it back, but Mama says if we rise up, something'll happen to us. We'll get beat up—maybe even lynched!"

She meant it. I'd known for some time that she was afraid of upsetting white folks by stepping out of line in even the smallest way. She'd been taught that there was no law on the side of blacks. So she'd learned to be afraid of whites. Earlier experiences in her life and in her family made her afraid to speak up when injustices were done.

One incident that happened to her when we were kids helped me understand why. She was waiting in an office in town when another woman there missed her ring. Later that day, after she got home, the sheriff came and arrested her. She was too scared to protest much. But the sheriff laid the "facts" out anyway: "Lucille, you have no husband, do you? And you needed the money, didn't you? So you took the ring and sold it, didn't you?" She told him no, but it didn't matter. He arrested her anyway and put her in jail.

This tore all of us apart. Mama was the matriarch of the family, the one holding it all together. And we were at a total loss to know how to respond or what to do. I stayed up crying all night, wondering whether or not I'd lost her through a system I didn't understand. It never entered my mind that she could be guilty. I knew she wasn't. I knew it was just the system—a system she feared because of things like that.

I remember feeling hopeless. I wondered, *Is there such a thing as justice? Is there anyone who has a caring, loving, concerned spirit? Or does everything happen at the whim of a dominant group? Is it always set up where if they said you did it, you must have done it?*

If so, the best thing you could do is not do it! But even then, who or what was stopping white folks from saying that you did? A sheriff could take Mama away just like that, on the merest suspicion, without any proof—just because some white person must have said Lucille had done it.

Furthermore, what happened to her from that moment on all depended on white folks. The next day the sheriff talked with some whites in our community about my mother. They told him she worked hard to feed her family, that she'd always been honest, and that it seemed unlikely she could be the thief. Because those folks said she was all right, the sheriff let her out of jail.

It was so typical of the system: If whites are against you, you're going to get the worst. If they're for you, you'll get by. You were almost forced to have a white who would vouch for you, who would "take care of you," or you couldn't survive. Who else was there to turn to? A lawyer? There were no black lawyers. And who could afford a white one? Who would trust him, either? He could just take your money and go into a room with a judge or the other lawyer and compromise you completely with you being out of the room.

So it was important to have white people who thought well of you, and especially of your work. Of course, this completely broke down any sense of justice. A black man might get to drinking and beat up his wife. Then he'd get arrested. And then he'd call his white boss to get him out of jail.

"Sure, Johnny gets a little drunk every weekend," the boss would argue. "Yeah, and maybe he hit his woman a few times. It happens. But man, come Monday morning he's the hardest workin' man I got! You can't keep him in jail just for a little domestic spat! I need him back on Monday to work!" And in no time the black man would be free. No justice for his wife!

These were not just isolated instances. A whole system was at work that kept blacks in their place. It was a system that dated all the way back to slavery.

I remember living three miles from Braxton. In the early years of this century, Braxton was known as a place where you just didn't want to be after sundown: "Don't get caught in Braxton," everyone warned. According to Mama, almost every Saturday night there had been a sick form of entertainment called "hanging a nigger."

Around 1915 my grandmother, Virgie Bell Granderson, was being courted by a young man who worked at the Braxton Hotel. He had Sundays off, and he came to see her. Every time he left to go back to Braxton, he said good-bye with the words, "I'll see you next Sunday—if I be livin'!"

He told her that in Braxton, all it took was for a black person to look at a white in the wrong way or to say the wrong thing, and he'd be lynched. That fellow rode the train at nights and always feared someone would get him when he got off the train. One night they did. They lynched him and wouldn't let anybody come and get the body.

There were more than five hundred documented lynchings in Mississippi before 1954. Braxton was known among blacks as one of the worst places for it. That sort of thing and the overall atmosphere surrounding it was an issue of power and control that some whites wanted to feel. They wanted to dominate the black person in every way possible. They used violence to do that. Lynching became a sport for some, a form of entertainment.

But the need for power extended even to small, day-to-day encounters between whites and blacks. Something as simple as talking to a white man face-to-face and looking him in the eye could be viewed as rebellious, as "a nigger not knowin' his place." If you said yes instead of yes sir, or no instead of no sir, you were out of line.

You also had to call a white man "Mr. John Smith," not just "John." You had to step out of the way when a white man or a white couple came by on the sidewalk. And if you were a black man, you never, never looked at a white woman or talked to her alone. If you violated any of these codes, you were asking for trouble. Of course, trouble could come to you anyway, whether you asked for it or not. It all depended on what a white person wanted.

Things got so bad that guys used to joke, "I was drivin' down to Mississippi and I got down to Tennessee. I got outta my car and started prayin', 'Lord, you know I'm scared. I'm gettin' ready to go into Mississippi, and I'm afraid. Lord, please go with me. Please give me a sign that you're goin' with me.'

"And the Lord says, 'Man, even I don't go into Mississippi!'"

It had been like that since slavery. Mama's great-grand-mother, Emily Dixon, had been a slave. They say she lived to be more than a hundred—to 112 or 118. She died in 1940. She was at least twenty-one at the time of Lincoln's Emancipation Proclamation, and, like the rest of the freed slaves, she was given forty acres and a mule to homestead. Later she willed this land to her granddaughter—my mother's mother. Mama had a number of years to be around her, and she passed down many stories about slavery.

"Great-grandma stayed with us a long time," Mama told us. "She walked with a stick. Her hair was plumb white, and her hands were hard-workin' hands, like a man's. She told us she had a good master and mistress, named Dixon. They never did whip her, like many of the slaveowners did to their slaves.

"Some of them were incredibly mean. They'd have babies by the black girls. Then speculators from the North would come down and buy the slaves. The bosses would sell off the mothers and leave the babies for the white mistress to raise. Great-grandma heard it told that one mistress took her foot and pushed a baby down the steps—I'm tellin' it just like Great-grandma told me! That woman would set him some milk and bread in a pan, and he'd have to come eat it like a dog! She'd throw a quilt in a corner where that baby would sleep, until it could grow up and walk.

"The bosses would beat some of the black men till their shirts were sticking to them with blood. But Great-grandma's

37

mistress was a good woman. She'd take lard and grease their backs."

The more I heard about what slavery was like from my mother and her stories from her great-grandmother, the more rage I felt. It wasn't a personal anger, but more a sense of outrage over what people went through—what my ancestors went through—under that system.

When the book *Roots* was made into the successful TV mini-series, it was a very important experience for us as blacks. It took that tragic experience and somehow transformed it into a deep, positive experience of pride. The feeling was that as a people, we survived a terrible thing, similar to the way many Jews survived Nazi Germany.

I especially took pride in the fact that Mama had direct contact with a slave. I own those roots. It's almost a badge of honor. When I talk about slavery, it's not in the abstract, not just something I've read about in a book. It's an experience passed directly to my mother and from her to me. It's something I pass on to my own children today.

But as a teenager thinking about what I was going to do with my life, I didn't feel any pride in being black. I'm surprised I didn't just end up angry. Certainly all the reasons were there why I should. I'd heard the stories about Mama's great-grandma as a slave. I'd heard about the lynching of my grandma's boyfriend by the men in Braxton. I'd seen my own mother locked up in jail for no reason. I'd been cheated myself by white farmers.

I knew the system was hopelessly stacked against me. No matter what I might do, nothing was going to change. The only way out, it seemed to me, was the one so many blacks took, the one so many of my friends and family took—to go somewhere else and start all over. Just forget Mississippi.

I got a lot of encouragement that way from my brother Melvin up in D.C. I visited him there, and guys would sit around talking about how glad they were to be out. "We can do whatever we want, man! We can go where we want to go. We can get any kind of car. We can get jobs and make some real money. And nobody can tell us what to do.

"But look at what you got in Mississippi. Even if you went to college and became something, so what? You become a doc-

tor—who's gonna let you practice? You become a teacher—
you're only gonna get to teach in the poor schools, with no pay.
It's hopeless.

"And what happens if you're drivin' down the road and a
bunch of white guys decide to stop you and take you out and
castrate you and beat you up, and maybe even lynch you?
Nothin' is gonna be done to them! Nothin' at all! In fact, they'll
probably be praised in the community!"

I believed they were right. The situation in Mississippi was
hopeless. I was only one person. I couldn't change it. So all I
wanted was to get out and live my life. I didn't know how I'd get
out. But I swore, "Someday I will! And when I do—I ain't never
comin' back!"

F I V E

A WAY OUT

VIA BASKETBALL

It was one thing to decide I was going to leave Mississippi.
Figuring out *how* was something else. I had no developed
skills, no money, not even a high school diploma yet. Still, my
mind was made up. So every day I played different schemes
over and over in my head, thinking about how to get out.

Then one day my life took an unexpected twist. A haircut
started everything. As I sat in the chair, my barber friend,
Leonard Stapleton, surprised me by asking, "Dolphus, are you
a Christian?"

I blinked, smiled, and finally shrugged. "I guess so. I'm doing
what everybody else is doing—going to church, trying to live
right. Sure, I think I'm a Christian."

"You can know for sure," he said in his quiet way. "You just
got to ask Jesus to come into your life."

It all sounded strangely familiar. His question rekindled all
those old feelings of inadequacy about religion, the fears that
I could never be good enough. I thought I'd buried all that in
the activity and friendships of adolescence. Now it was staring
me in the face again.

Yet something felt curiously different. Maybe it was the way
Leonard had asked me the question. Maybe it was the idea that
you could somehow be *sure* that you were right with God. I felt

the faintest tingle of hope that maybe Leonard knew something about religion I didn't.

So when he invited me to come to a tent meeting to find out
more, I said yes. I doubted it would be much different from the
revival meetings at my church. But again, I hoped that maybe,
just maybe, this time would be different.

I also was curious when I heard who was leading it—John
Perkins of the Voice of Calvary ministry in Mendenhall. Rev.
Perkins had spoken a few times in chapel service at Harper
High School, the school I attended. He also worked with black
kids in the community. Everybody respected him a lot because
he'd come back from California to establish a ministry for
blacks in Simpson County.

That fascinated me, since I was trying to leave Simpson
County. I often wondered why a guy who'd been a success
somewhere else would want to come back to Mendenhall. And
why would he want to change jobs and become a preacher?
For that matter, what I knew of Rev. Perkins didn't seem to fit
my image of black preachers. Everyone called him "John" instead of "Rev. Perkins." He lived simply, just like the rest of us.
And he walked around town in jeans and a shirt, just like the
rest of us. I thought, *If this guy's a preacher, where's his Cadillac?*

So I had a lot of interest when Leonard and I showed up to
the tent meeting that night. There were about sixty people
there. Mrs. Perkins was up front leading them in choruses. I
still remember singing "My Lord Knows the Way through the
Wilderness," "Deep and Wide," and "I Love Him Better Every
Day."

Then John got up and gave a short flannelgraph lesson. It
may sound strange to think of him using flannelgraph with
adults, but it was the only audiovisual available. Plus there
were a few children in the group, so it made it interesting for
them. In addition, John had a very engaging, believable personality, and the pictures just added to everything he was
saying.

The main speaker, though, was a Rev. Wallace, a fiery
preacher who moved around a lot on the platform. In the
middle of his message he began talking about a verse in the
Psalms (116:12) that said, "What shall I render to the LORD for
all His benefits toward me?"

He used the verse to talk about all the things that God has done for us. He also talked about how every person in the world is born a sinner and how because of sin we all deserve to be punished. He said God offers us eternal life as a gift, that He loves us and wants to free us from sin. Finally, he said that a person could receive eternal life just like he receives a gift—he doesn't have to do anything, just accept it from God. And then he invited anyone who wanted to receive eternal life to come up front and stand before him, and he'd tell us exactly how.

While he spoke, something clicked for me. All my life I'd worked hard to be good enough for God, "worked hard to make 100 percent," just like the song said. Yet I always felt that I fell short. But that night I suddenly realized that salvation was something God was willing to give me for free.

So along with three or four others, I went up to the front of the tent. Someone met me and explained that I could tell God directly that I realized I was a sinner, that I wanted His salvation, and that I accepted it as His gift to me. So I did. I was convinced it was true.

Leonard and I came back to the tent meetings every night for the rest of the week. Then on Tuesday of the following week, I started attending a Bible study at Voice of Calvary, where we talked about what had happened in more detail and looked at the Bible to see what it taught. For the first time in my life, someone was showing me the truths of Christianity in more than a superficial way.

But it was more than just classes. As I watched the folks associated with Voice of Calvary, I began to notice the difference Christ made in how they lived their lives. Herbert Jones, for instance, lived with the Perkinses and was a gentle giant of a man who always had a smile. I was struck with the way he always pitched in to help. If there was cleaning to be done, he'd clean. If a driver was needed, he'd drive. He'd get up early and stay up late to help people. He gave me a whole new light on what it meant to be a Christian. I'd always seen the preachers, the up-front folks as the real Christians. But Herbert showed me what it's like to be like Christ, who was willing to be a servant.

And then there was Mr. Buckley. He was already seventy-five back then, but he still had about twenty-five years left to his life. I identified with Mr. Buckley because of his experience in the faith. I talked with him one day about when he started out as a Christian.

"It was in 1904," he told me. He'd been attending a revival week. "In my time they had what they called a mourners' bench in front of the pulpit. After the preacher finished, they'd sing a song and say, 'Everybody who wants to be prayed for, come and get on this bench.' Just as soon as they began the song, I went up there. I said to God, 'I don't know how to present myself to You, but I heard the man, what he said about You, and now I want that.' I went from the first night to the last, on the mourners' bench. That was my prayer every night.

"The last night of the services they got up and sang a song to dismiss. And when they sang that song, something spoke to me. It said, 'You got all you'll ever have, what are you holdin' back on?' I asked, 'Will you wait and take me in?' They prayed for me. It's lasted all these years—gets stronger and stronger every day."

Mr. Buckley apparently understood enough about what this preacher was saying to ask Jesus to come into his life. And he became a faithful attender at church. However, he told me that for fifty years he'd looked for a church that preached the Bible and was concerned about people's needs, but they all fell short in some way.

As a result, he had nobody to teach him how to live as a Christian. Still, he acted on what little he knew. So when John Perkins came to town, Mr. Buckley responded right away by saying, "This is the first time I've ever heard anybody get into the meat of the Bible! I've been looking for it all these years, and finally I've found someone who can give it to me!"

Mr. Buckley was right. John was a completely different sort of minister. His faith made a difference. It went beyond emotionalism. It was a faith attached to reality. He tied it to voting, to politics, to poverty, to the here and now. That made him very attractive to black folks in Simpson County.

And the more I got to know him, the more believable he became. I learned that he'd grown up in Mississippi, too, in a background somewhat like mine. He'd never made it past third grade. His family couldn't read or write. Worst of all, he'd seen his brother shot and killed on the streets of New Hebron, all because he no longer "knew his place" with white folks, having returned from World War II, where race didn't matter much on the battlefield.

All of this gave birth to tremendous rage in John, so he packed up his family and left for California lest his anger get him in trouble. If hopelessness was driving me out of Mississippi, hatred had driven John out.

Yet something unexpected happened to him in California. Through an amazing series of circumstances, John had turned his life over to Christ. He began to study the Bible. And God began to do some phenomenal things in his attitude and character.

One of the things John started doing as a new Christian was visiting prisons and speaking about the gospel. He quickly realized that more than half the inmates were black. Moreover, he discovered that an unusually large number of those men had come from Alabama, Georgia, Louisiana—and Mississippi.

They were guys who'd tried to escape the racism of the old South. But they couldn't cope in a new system. They had no skills, little education, no money, and no way to get a decent job. So to make ends meet they'd turned to crime, and they ended up in jail.

When John saw that, he decided that the place to address that problem was not in California prisons but in the hamlets of the deep South. He decided to start up a ministry to reach people, especially young people, before they got that far. So he came back to Mississippi and started Voice of Calvary.

I respected him for that choice. It wasn't the one I would have made. Here was a guy who'd had it made in California. He'd had a good job and was moving up in his company. He'd just bought a thirteen-room house, and his wife and kids loved it. But he had such a desire to see things change, to make a difference. It was a commitment that flowed out of his devotion to Christ. I found that very attractive.

I guess John was attracted to me, too, because one day he said, "Dolphus, I'm going back out to California for a couple of weeks to visit some friends. Why don't you come with me?" I asked Mama, and she didn't have any problem with it. As long as I was with Rev. Perkins, she knew I'd be OK.

So in the summer before my senior year of high school I drove with the Perkins family to California. Except for my father's funeral in Louisiana, it was the only time I'd ever left Mississippi. We drove through Texas. John knew all the right places to stop along the way. Only occasionally did we get stuck in some little town that had no restrooms for blacks.

When I got to California and saw the orange orchards and the ocean and all, it was like an impossible dream come true. I just wondered, *What am I doing out here? This is something!* It was a fascinating experience for this farm boy.

We spent time visiting folks who'd been friends to John and supported him in his ministry. I got to meet people who'd helped him get started as a Christian, and they were very encouraging to me. One lady, Mrs. Adair, seemed to think I showed a lot of promise. So she gave me a gift—a brand new *Scofield Reference Bible.* I was stunned by her faith in me and deeply appreciative of her gift. It was the first Bible I ever owned. I treasure it to this day.

In the fall I started my senior year at Harper High School. It was called a high school, but it also had elementary and junior high grades. There were five or six hundred kids—all black.

When basketball season started, I was in my element. We had a good team. Our problem was McLaurin, one of two other black high schools in Simpson County. McLaurin had a super team. Our claim to fame was that both times we played them that year, we held them to beating us by only seven points. We were the only team to do that.

The other school in the county was New Hymn. One time the seniors from Harper played the seniors at New Hymn. That game turned out to be one of the most important in my life. At half time we were beating them on their own court, 45 to 12. It was a joke! So they asked if their coach could play with them. He had been a star player at Mississippi's largest black college. We said OK.

Ten minutes later, we were in a whole new ball game! Our guys were still shooting OK from the floor, but defensively we were in trouble. Their coach scored again and again. And their players, instead of looking grim, were getting excited. Their home court crowd was screaming as the player-coach cut our lead to two points.

With thirty seconds left, they called time out. The goal was for him to hold the ball and take the last shot. So we went into a man-to-man defense. Since I'd always thought I was a good defensive player, I wanted him. I knew that the one thing in the world he wanted was to make that shot, tie the score, and send the game into overtime. He dodged left—I was there! He looked around for a chance to pass—no way! He dribbled down the court—I took after him! The clock ticked down to five seconds. When he finally went for the shot, I went up with him. I was a great jumper. He changed his shot in midair, the ball hit the rim—and bounced away!

The crowd went wild! They wanted to stone us! But then something incredible happened. We were all heading for the locker room when this coach from New Hymn came up and put his hand on my shoulder and said, "Have you ever thought about playing college ball?"

He might as well have sucker-punched me! What with the noise and the emotion of the moment and all, I thought maybe he was joking. But when I looked into his eyes, I could tell he was serious. And the significant thing was the touch—just a real sense of confidence and respect he communicated to me. My own coach had never said or done anything like that.

But I immediately started thinking up all kinds of excuses why it couldn't happen. "Me? No way! I'm too short. And I don't have a very good outside jump shot. And I'd have to switch to guard. And . . ." I was going down a list of objections.

But the guy kept talking to me there in the hall. And for the first time in my life, I started feeling that maybe I did have what it took to play college ball. If I did, I might be able to use that as a way to pay my tuition.

This was a new and incredible idea to me. It was a different perspective on basketball than a lot of black kids have today. They see these superstars on professional basketball teams and think, *Man, that's what I want to become! That's the ticket out of my hopeless situation.* But they don't understand. They think that because they're the hottest kid on the court and can beat every kid on the block, they have world-class potential. The problem is, they never get a correct assessment of their skills.

Every major university, every college that has a ball club, has a star—every one of them. But when you start talking about becoming a professional, you have to consider that less than fifty kids a year come out of college and make it in the NBA. If you don't assess your skills properly and keep things in perspective, you can waste a lot of time dreaming about something that will never happen.

When I looked at myself, I never saw NBA lights. I just realized, *Boy! Maybe I can use my talent to pay for college education! That's got a future to it! Praise God!*

From that day on, I set my heart on attending Mississippi Valley State College. Congress had put a lot of pressure on Mississippi to demonstrate its "separate but equal" doctrine. So the state had finally allotted money to upgrade the inadequate facilities of the black colleges under its jurisdiction. At Mississippi Valley the new concrete-block buildings that emerged from flat delta farmlands looked like Harvard to me! I was determined to be there in the fall!

Finally I graduated from Harper, first in my class. Within two weeks, 75 percent of my classmates had left Mississippi, most of them for good. None of them wanted to go through life as a maid or a sharecropper. I couldn't blame them. I was planning to get out, too—after college.

But first I went to see my brother Melvin in Washington, D.C. He was working at the time for a food processing company, packing precooked food for shipment to restaurants. I got a job, too, and worked hard to save everything I could. But when it was time to come home, I had only three hundred dollars, six hundred short of what I needed to enroll. In a panic I applied for a loan, but my application was too late. I didn't know anything about work-study programs, and I had no one to write or call and say, "I need help." So once again, despite my hard work and desire, it looked like I was shut out.

All was not lost, however. My buddy, Jimmie Walker, had accepted a basketball scholarship to Prentiss Institute. When he found out what had happened, he started telling me about Prentiss and how they had a National Defense Student Loan program, and you could borrow whatever you needed to go to school. So I ended up going there with Jimmie. But then one day I figured out how much the loan was costing me each year, and I wondered whether it was worth it for the level of training Prentiss could offer.

So I began to talk about leaving Prentiss. About the same time, my high school coach arranged an appointment with the coach at Piney Woods Junior College. We met and he got real enthusiastic. Finally he promised me, "Dolphus, if you come up here, I'll get you a scholarship." That really got my attention! But in addition, I was drawn to the school because of its philosophy of education, emphasizing "head, heart, and hands."

Dr. Laurence C. Jones founded the school in 1909 and remained its president until 1974. He was a real hero in the black community. But his idea of educating blacks struck fear in the white community. They thought he was out to train their niggers to be "uppity" by learning to read, and they were afraid of losing their farmhands—and their control. They got so upset that one night they captured Dr. Jones, planning to lynch him.

The story goes that while he sat on the horse with his head in the noose, he took charge of the mob by explaining himself: "My goal is to give people a head knowledge, so they'll know how to read and take care of your children. I want to give them a heart knowledge so they'll know about the Lord and be submissive to Him. And I want to give them a hand knowledge so they'll be better farmers and better carpenters and better plumbers and better electricians. I'm doing this for your sakes as much as for theirs."

I guess it impressed the crowd because they backed down and let him go. Later he appeared on TV on "This Is Your Life" with Ralph Edwards. At the end of the show, after reviewing Dr. Jones' remarkable life and the story of Piney Woods, Edwards told the audience that if everyone would send in just one dollar, Piney Woods could go a long way toward being permanently endowed. More than a million dollars poured in, plus the mailing list swelled to a half-million.

I wanted to be in a place with that kind of legacy, that kind of electricity! So I dropped out of Prentiss, packed my bags, and headed up to Piney Woods—only to learn that I had never been registered! What was worse, the school was already overcrowded! In his enthusiasm, the basketball coach had never worked out the details for enrollment or a scholarship. And I'd been foolish enough to just take his word for it. I didn't know how the system worked. So I was out of luck.

I was also out of work and out of ideas on how to get going on a college education. So I took the first job that came along, laying sewage pipe in a little delta town called Anguilla. My work was in a trench six feet deep, putting braces in to hold it open and laying the pipe. The longer I worked on that job, the worse I felt about myself and my situation. There I was, down there in that ditch, making less than half of what the white supervisor up on the bank was making. He'd come by and dirt would crumble off and fall on my back. From dawn until late in the afternoon I'd labor, with only a handful of five- or ten-minute breaks. And the boss man was always threatening to fire me if I didn't work faster.

Then, twice a day, I'd look up and see the school bus drive by and feel the rumble in the earth as it passed. That really hurt! I'd think, *Hey, Dolphus, didn't you graduate valedictorian? Weren't you voted Most Likely to Succeed? What're you doing in this ditch? For that matter, what're you doing in this one-horse town, living in a slum, making slave wages in a hole?* I really thrashed myself!

I felt like I was getting sucked back into the old cycle of poverty that I'd grown up in. I thought back to all the pain and hard times of growing up poor. And I just hated it. I was ashamed of it—ashamed of the house I'd grown up in, ashamed of the clothes I'd had and the ones I didn't have, ashamed of the food I'd had to eat, ashamed of picking cotton, and especially ashamed of getting cheated by white folks. It all felt very hopeless. I'd come so close to rising above it. Was I going to lose out now?

In the end I decided that the only way out was to somehow get an education, and if I didn't get back in school right away, I never would. So I went back to Piney Woods to see if they might have any openings at the end of the quarter, which was in November. When they told me they definitely had a place, I hurried over to the coach to claim my basketball scholarship. By the start of the second quarter, I was on my way!

Still, missing that first quarter hurt me academically. When I told my white English teacher, Miss Gillespie, that I needed to make up the first quarter, she offered to help. That encouraged me to ask other teachers if I could make up the subjects they taught. I played catch-up in about four courses—a lot of work, but anything was better than laying sewer pipe! Soon I was back on schedule.

Piney Woods had a number of extracurricular requirements that benefited me. For example, I had to learn a trade. I chose dry-cleaning. I was fascinated by the process as well as the product—clean, bright clothes! Speech-making was also required, so I learned how to handle myself before a group. In fact, by my second year at Piney Woods, I became president of the Collegiate Commentators' Club, which brought issues for debate before the student body.

Being in an academic setting, I became more aware of social and political issues and the people behind them. I learned a lot more about the burgeoning civil rights movement and the hope that it offered black people. I also kept myself informed on the ugly things that were happening. Black marchers and whites who supported them were killed in Alabama, while closer to home in Jackson, Medgar Evers was gunned down on the doorstep of his home. His death made me stop and think about my own life and how dangerous it had become to be a black in Mississippi. I knew it could happen to me. In response, I renewed my determination to get out of the state as soon as I finished at Piney Woods.

I began to hope that I could go to a Christian college somewhere else for my last two years of school. I felt a growing conviction that ultimately I belonged in some kind of ministry. But I didn't want to become a traditional black preacher like the ones I'd known growing up. I wanted to be able to handle the truth of the Bible with clarity and integrity. I also wanted to deal with the needs of the whole person in practical ways.

My role model, of course, was John Perkins. His ministry in Mendenhall was moving forward. During the mornings he farmed, and in the afternoons and evenings he led Bible studies and other activities at schools in four counties. He also visited people's homes to read the Bible, pray, and help in whatever way he could.

He bought a piece of property in the black section of Mendenhall and contracted with a builder to complete the shell of a house. Then a bunch of us, including Herbert Jones, my brother Melvin, Artis Fletcher, a Bible school student, myself, and others, finished out the inside for the Perkins family to finally have a home in the community.

I liked the way that John was interested in living among us in the neighborhood instead of up in Jackson or some place where he could only visit occasionally. It was one more contrast between his style of ministry and the other black preachers I'd known.

Another thing that impressed me about John was how much he'd done with the little he had to start with. His background had been much like mine, yet he'd made something of himself, so much so that he had a lot to give to other people.

I realized that all my life I'd been ashamed of myself and my background. But one day at school the Lord impressed me with the thought that it's not so important who you are but who you become. You have no control over what family you're born into or what level of education they have or what kind of house you're raised in. You have nothing to do with where you start out. But you have a lot of control over what you make of yourself over time.

I thought about Mama, with her tattered clothes and a house falling down around her. And I thought of how she took what she had and did the best she could with it—and she did awfully well! She'd raised nine kids, kept us fed and clothed, got us educated, got us started in life, built some real values in us. It just filled me with pride for her. And so I realized that for me to be ashamed of the external things was foolish. What mattered was what you become, not where you start.

That was a breakthrough for me. I'd hit bottom while I was digging ditches. Now I took pride in myself, and dedicated myself to becoming the best person I could be, with God's help. I began to challenge other students at Piney Woods with the same outlook, especially the ones who, like me, came from poor backgrounds.

I also developed a vague idea that I wanted to so something similar to John and the others at the ministry. I didn't know what, but I wanted to prepare for it as best I could. To me that meant finishing my education at a Christian college. There was just one problem—I didn't know of a single accredited four-year Christian college that would admit a black person. I knew some Bible institutes that educated blacks. But I wanted a full college education as well as Bible instruction.

One day during my second year at Piney Woods, a group of young men from California spoke in chapel. John Perkins had arranged for them to talk about their lives and their vision for ministry. When they invited students to talk with them after chapel, I went up and introduced myself.

"Hello, Dolphus," one of them said, shaking my hand. "I'm David Nicholas, director of admissions at Los Angeles Baptist College and Seminary. And this is John MacArthur, a student at Talbot Seminary." As we talked, I explained that I, too, was a Christian who wanted to go into the ministry. After a while, John asked, "Do you plan to continue college after you finish at Piney Woods?"

I paused, wondering what to tell him. "I'd like to go to a Christian college," I said, "but I don't know any that accept blacks."

David stunned me by replying, "How would you like to attend Los Angeles Baptist College?" I was at a loss to know how to respond. On the one side I knew I wanted a good education, and this school sounded pretty good. I also wanted to get out of Mississippi, and I remembered how much I'd enjoyed California before. But, faced with the prospect of attending a white college outside Mississippi, I wondered whether I could compete academically. Suddenly I felt very afraid. I don't know whether it showed, but the two men kept talking about the college as though they didn't notice.

So I threw them an obstacle to see how serious they were. "I don't have any money. I'd need a loan, or maybe a basketball scholarship."

"OK, I'll talk to the coach and maybe we can get you one," David replied. "He'll get in touch with you. I think he'll be real interested. We're building a new gym on campus and trying to strengthen our basketball program."

That sounded great! Still, my old feelings of inferiority made me skeptical that it could really happen—or that I could perform if it did.

But when a letter and scholarship offer came from the coach, I finally had to decide. Everything I ever wanted was suddenly within my grasp: a complete college education, paid for by a basketball scholarship; training in the Bible in preparation for ministry; a school that accepted blacks as well as whites; and most of all, a chance to finally get free of Mississippi. Why, then, was I so afraid?

Fortunately I wasn't alone in the situation. John Perkins had told Jimmie Walker about LABC, urging him to go there as well. Jimmie had also been offered a basketball scholarship. So we got together to talk things over.

"I want to go, but I'm scared!" I admitted.

"You're scared! Man, I'm scared, too!" he said. "At least you've been to California."

"Well, we wanted to leave Mississippi, didn't we?"

"Yeah, but what if we don't make it?"

"You mean the academics?"

"Yeah, and maybe even the basketball. What if we don't make the team?"

All the self-doubt, fear, and inferiority that we'd grown up with were lashing us with a fury, beating us down. It was as if the entire weight of the system was fighting against us in an all-out effort to keep us forever chained in hopelessness.

But somewhere in the confusion, I felt the strong arm of the New Hymn coach on my shoulder, and the power of his words: "Why don't you play college ball?" I realized that the only thing standing in my way was me. What was I waiting for? Besides, I had Jimmie to go with me. Finally I resolved to go for it and turned to him and said, "I'll go if you'll go!" So we did.

SIX

BREAKING THE BARRIERS

IN AN

ALL-WHITE COLLEGE

Jimmie and I arrived at Los Angeles Baptist College in August of 1967. Pete Reese, our new basketball coach, and a dorm resident assistant welcomed us with a tour of the campus. We got real excited by the new gym. Two years earlier, LABC had had a team with a record of four wins and eighteen losses. The next year they recruited a six-foot-ten player and improved to seven and sixteen. Now we talked it up about how this year we'd go twenty-four straight!

"So, Coach," I finally asked, "where are some of the other black students?"

He kind of looked funny and then said, "Well, there aren't any others. You two are the first to live on campus and go to school here full-time."

I suddenly felt sick to my stomach. My mind flashed back to the invitation of David Nicholas to apply. I'd just assumed that LABC was an integrated Christian college. Never in my wildest imagination had I thought that we were going to be the pioneers in integrating it! I'd seen how integration worked—or didn't work—in Mississippi. I wasn't at all sure that I wanted to be the point man here in breaking down racial barriers.

But what could we do? We were stuck, and we had to make the best of it. So finally I said, "OK, why don't you just show us our room, and we'll get settled."

That's when the RA piped up. "Uh, that's something else you need to know. You guys won't be rooming together."

"What?" Jimmie and I reeled from the second shock of the day. "But that means—"

"You'll each have a white roommate," the coach finished, reading our minds. Then he went on: "The white students know about it, and they've agreed."

That's just great, I thought. *Nobody asked us what we want to do! But the whites had consented—like they're doing us a favor!* I felt disgusted.

I also felt confused. Why would a white guy even consider rooming with a black? It would never happen that way in Mississippi! Maybe it was good that the whites knew what was coming. At least that way they wouldn't be as surprised as we were when we found out!

I knew I was supposed to feel good about being able to attend LABC, but a nagging skepticism made me interpret these whites' gesture as, "We're doing you a favor whether you like it or not!"

Jimmie and I ditched our stuff in our respective rooms and walked off campus to see the town of Newhall, where LABC was located. About thirty miles north of L.A. near the San Fernando Valley, the town had about fourteen thousand people. And the more we walked and looked around, the more we realized they were fourteen thousand *white* people! Finally, we just had to laugh. Not only were we the only blacks at LABC— we were the only blacks in town! I think three or four months passed before either of us saw another black face.

Still, the racial climate was very different from Simpson County. Somehow, as we walked around, we didn't feel black. We didn't feel like second-class citizens, mostly because no one seemed to treat us that way. That gave us some hope.

And we sure needed it! When I got back to my dorm, I stopped for a moment on the steps and looked out at the hills surrounding Newhall. They were dry and brown and hot and dusty! I suddenly caught myself longing for the cool green fields and woods of Mississippi. I was in a strange place. I was alone. And I was downright scared. I was already homesick. I just kept thinking, *Man, what have I done? What in the world am I doing here?*

The time had come to meet my roommate, so I went on inside. Dave Button, the son of one of the professors, was a real cordial guy. I was surprised at how well we hit it off right away. I knew he'd been primed that I was black, but I found out that he'd wanted to be my roommate, and that he was really open to giving and taking and learning. He turned out to be a valuable asset in those early days at LABC.

The same was true with Jimmie's roommate, John Appel. The four of us spent a lot of time together and became good friends. We all relaxed and got to the point where it was OK to blunder, to say something stupid, to ask a dumb question. I remember Jimmie used shaving powder called Magic Shave. It smelled like rotten eggs! He'd be in the bathroom, shaving, and guys would smell it and yell, "Man, what is that stuff!" We'd kid him and make jokes. It really helped everybody loosen up.

We didn't completely forget about our image as blacks, though. We decided to accept the challenge to be pioneers in overcoming stereotypes. We had a lot going for us in that we were upperclassmen, and basketball players to boot. But we still took care what we said and how we acted. We stayed away from the rowdy guys who were always bending the rules. And we never dared to date white girls. We'd been told up front that that was a no-no.

In a way we walked a tightrope, trying to mix in, yet trying to remain distinctive. We decided that our main goal was to get an education, and we didn't want anything to interfere with that, least of all our race. So we put up with some minor inconveniences.

Like our appearance. Those were the days of Black Power, the raised fist, the new black militancy. The TV was showing speeches by guys like Stokely Carmichael and H. Rap Brown that just scared the whites around us and made them angry. We certainly understood the context and the symbolism behind the Black Power movement. But we disagreed with its agenda of violence.

To distance ourselves from all of that, we intentionally cut our hair shorter than we would have liked. And I shaved my mustache. That seems so minor now, but it was a big thing then. In short, we made our choices based on the goal of getting through school, as well as a feeling that we were paving the way for other blacks to attend white colleges.

Another area where we really had to work ourselves was academics. As soon as classes started, we realized we were way behind everyone else. But we made up our minds to persevere. For instance, I'd never even heard of calculus, so I went out and bought *Calculus Made Simple* and struggled through extra work. I was determined to compete on a level with any student there.

One day near the end of the first semester, my history professor made an announcement to our class of about seventy students. "The top ten students are excused from the exam, so if I call your name, you can leave before I explain to the rest what to expect on the test."

He went down the list, calling out names. Most of the kids were talking and carrying on. Suddenly he called, "Dolphus Weary." Everybody stopped chattering and the room got so quiet I could hear my heart beating. I'd just shattered the stereotype of being black and dumb! Later I realized how that incident revealed what my classmates thought of my academic ability. But more important, it showed me what I needed to think about myself!

When basketball season started, Jimmie and I came into our element. The coach put together a first-rate team, and we won six consecutive games. The whole campus was on a high! Everybody thought we were tremendous. By the end of the season, we placed nineteen victories and only five defeats.

But I began to notice something about all the smiles and backslapping from the other students. It felt great, but often it masked what they really felt. We couldn't always get the truth from people. Many were probably afraid of us. That was understandable. But we also ran into clear-cut cases of racism, both subtle and obvious.

A lot of it was petty stuff—racial jokes, teasing about the way blacks talk, comments about our hair. That didn't bother us too much. After all, differences in themselves aren't bad—they're just differences, and it seems fairly harmless to laugh at them. But there was also a small group of students who just wouldn't speak to us. They apparently had made up their minds to act as if we didn't exist, or as if we were a problem that would go away.

There was a more active group, however, that seemed to want to challenge our right to equal treatment. I remember one time somebody asked us, "You know, this theory of evolution—is it true that you all came from monkeys?" That was pretty vicious. But then some other kids brought to campus a documentary film that tried to prove that the black people involved in the civil rights movement were communists!

This kind of abuse put a lot of pressure on us. Fortunately we knew a lot about handling pressure from our experience with basketball. But it was hard not to get angry and lash out. It hurt to feel that kind of prejudice, and it was also confusing. Back home we'd concluded that there were no white Christians in Mississippi, since in our limited world we rarely encountered whites who treated black people with anything but contempt. Now we were shocked to find that white Christians in California were not above racist attitudes.

Things hit bottom one day when somebody came up and told me, "Martin Luther King just got shot!"

"What?" I cried. "You're kidding!" I ran to my room and flipped on the radio. The newscasters were talking about it. I was devastated. I started praying, listening to the reports as they came in, churned up over what it could mean.

As I sat there on my bed, I overheard voices down the hall, talking about it—talking about how glad they were that Martin Luther King had been shot! *What am I hearing?* I wondered incredulously. *What is this? Am I in a foreign country? I thought this was America! I thought this was a Christian school, and here are these kids talking about how glad they are that Martin Luther King's been shot!*

This went on for a while. My first impulse was to rush out and confront them. These kids were sick! Furthermore, I believed that by laughing at Martin Luther King, they were laughing at me, and at all the other millions of black people that Martin Luther King spoke for. But I resisted that. I needed to get control. I felt nauseous. I was hurt, disillusioned, and angry.

Then the report came: "Martin Luther King has died in a Memphis hospital." A cheer erupted from the group down the hall. I couldn't tell who it was—I didn't want to. I just kept wondering, *Isn't this supposed to be a Christian school? How can we even think about being happy over anyone's death? Even if it's Khrushchev or Fidel Castro, how can we possibly be cheering or jumping for joy?*

I felt tired. I was tired of dealing with the kind of racist idiocy exhibited by the kids down the hall. I was exhausted, too, from my vigil of waiting for word on Dr. King. I'd never met him personally, but I had enormous regard for him. He was calling America to rethink itself, to look at its use of power, and in particular to reflect on its treatment of a certain segment of its people.

He was trying to get all of us to open our eyes and see injustice. He was talking about racism and segregation, not just in the white community, but in the black community as well. He was pointing out all the different kinds of slavery that still existed, at a time when it wasn't popular to speak ill of America.

So he'd become a role model for me. I identified with him as a hero with a mission. For him to have gone through all that he did, he had to have a sense of mission. Not so much a religious mission—sometimes my conservative Christian brothers would want me to nail down on whether Dr. King was an "evangelical," a "real" Christian. I felt he was a Christian, though I wouldn't have called him an "evangelical." His was the mission of a prophet, calling people to repentance in relation to the sins of racism and injustice.

And the amazing thing was that he had influenced people without resorting to violence. That was an inspiration to me, change occurring in a nonviolent way. He was our hope. But with word of his death, hope seemed to die, too.

I was glad my roommate wasn't there just then. But suddenly I thought of Jimmie, and I sort of woke up. Jimmie and I needed each other. I found him in his room, listening to the radio. Neither of us spoke. We didn't need to. After a while I told him what I'd overheard from my dorm room. He shook his head, disgusted, but not surprised. We talked into the night—the only two blacks for miles around.

We decided that we had to formulate a response, a strategy for handling ourselves in this moment of crisis. We realized that hate was not the answer. Hate directs your anger toward an entire group, which is unfair. If anger needs to be expressed, it needs to be aimed at particular individuals who are off base, not at white people as a whole. That was part of the problem with the Black Power movement. It wanted to tear the whole society down, not correct the evils by and through whatever strengths there were in the system.

We also prayed, and I believe God spoke to us out of the muddle of our questions and feelings on that terrible night. He showed us that the problem was much bigger and more basic than a handful of jokers sounding off in a hallway. They were just acting out of the ignorance and bigotry passed on to them by families who'd never dealt with the problem of prejudice. That kind of prejudice could only be overcome by His power. But He could use us in a powerful way to open doors of understanding. In a sense, we could become teachers as well as students on a campus dominated by white people.

In light of this, we decided to become more active in speaking up and setting the terms of the discussion. Wherever an opportunity might exist to speak out on behalf of black needs and issues, we needed to find the courage to do so. In this way we could stimulate dialogue and get whites involved with us in overcoming problems.

A good place to start, we decided, was with our own roommates. So I finally returned to my room and poured out my hurt and anger to Dave. We talked for a long time. He felt bad about the actions of the kids down the hall, but he had no answer for their behavior.

In the weeks that followed, I acted on my resolve to talk openly about prejudice. Instead of avoiding controversy, I created it—not by being rude, but by encouraging kids around me to discuss their attitudes about racial and civil rights issues. When people asked questions that raised such issues, I responded—not with the old soft answers, but with more information. If I had a chance to make a speech in class, I made sure it was about a black person or a black concern. When a paper was assigned, I wrote on subjects like the history of the black church or the relationship of the white church to slavery. Each time I spoke in chapel, I addressed questions of prejudice and racism, trying to break down stereotypes and create an awareness of black worth.

This activism became my mission during that spring semester. I felt it was my job to help the students and professors around me understand what black Americans were saying. Otherwise they might leave that institution and embrace the same mentality as those kids who were laughing. Furthermore, as people who would take on leadership in their churches, they would influence countless others. Would theirs be an influence toward open-mindedness? Or would the churches keep on looking at poverty and injustice and say they were someone else's fault and therefore someone else's responsibility?

I'll never know how much I accomplished by these efforts. But as I accompanied my actions with prayer, I began to see breakthroughs with some of the students by the end of the school year. That lifted my hopes. King's dream of whites and blacks living in peace could become a reality after all. And I saw that I could be an agent of change and reconciliation.

At any rate, these small victories made the end of my first year at LABC much sweeter than the beginning. As Jimmie and I flew east on our way home for the summer, we thought back on how much had happened—and how far we'd come!

We also looked forward to getting back home to the piney green woods of Simpson County, to John Perkins and our friends at Voice of Calvary, and to our families. We had lots of stories to tell, lots of lessons we'd learned. We were eager to report on it all.

At Dallas's Love Field we changed planes for the final leg to Jackson. As we walked through the terminal, a female announcer's voice came over the public address: "Delta Airlines Flight 277 will depart from Gate 12 at four o'clock."

Something in the way she said *four*—a slight drawl, a Southern bending of the word into two syllables—called up a wave of associations. Suddenly I realized I was back in the South— and about to fly into the heart of the Deep South! As I walked that long corridor in the airport, I felt like I was changing roles from a college kid with a future to a Mississippi black boy who'd better know his place! What saved me at that moment was a reminder to myself that I was only going home for a visit— thank goodness, not to stay!

S E V E N

SUMMER MINISTRIES,

COLLEGE CHANGES—

AND ENGAGEMENT

As soon as Jimmie and I got home from California, we started telling everyone about our experience as "pioneers" on an all-white campus. That gave us a lot of stature in the community, and we felt a new responsibility to take leadership for helping blacks there in Mississippi. We were especially interested in doing something for kids, to give them a vision for their lives instead of the hopelessness they were growing up with.

One day as we sat around talking, John Perkins of Voice of Calvary ministry made a suggestion. "Dolphus, why don't you start a program right here in Simpson County?" We began to think about what we could do, and we settled on the idea of running vacation Bible school for churches in the area. I became the director of the program and recruited three high school seniors to help me.

We went to the churches and offered to run the program for their kids. If they would provide the buildings and the publicity, we would provide the teachers and the material. In the end, fourteen churches signed up for the service. So we held one vacation Bible school in the morning at one church, and another in the afternoon at another church. In this way we were able to expose scores of black kids in Simpson County to the gospel. We also tried to inject a sense of direction and hope into their lives. We also began to identify kids who looked like potential leaders.

We didn't limit this recruitment process to children. Jimmie and I began challenging college-age kids to apply to LABC and come to California with us in the fall. We thought LABC would be recruiting more blacks to the student body, but for whatever reason they weren't. We had other plans, though. We wanted as many qualified blacks as possible. It would do a lot for our cause there. But just as important, it would do a lot for the black students and the community they came from.

One of the women who ended up going to LABC was Carolyn Albritton. She had come to help in the ministry at Mendenhall that summer and was one of the first to apply. It was a breakthrough for all of us when she heard back from the school that she'd been accepted.

Carolyn invited a friend, Rosie Camper, to visit one week. I knew her because her father had driven the school bus when I was in high school. Rosie had responded to the gospel under John's ministry during her senior year of high school, and she had just graduated. She worked with us as we traveled to the county's rural churches to teach vacation Bible schools. She also joined us for prayer and Bible studies. One day she exclaimed, "You guys are really something! My family prayed some at home and even went to church a lot. But people at our church didn't seem concerned about anything except attendance and paying dues. Nobody witnessed or studied the Bible the way you do!" When she expressed her eagerness to learn more of the Bible, the Perkinses invited her to stay for the summer and continue to work with us.

We had a lot in common. All of us had grown up in rural Mississippi. And all of us at some point had realized how different our lives were from those of the white people around us. One day we were talking about how those differences had affected us.

"Truckloads of white guys used to drive by, hauling pulpwood from the woods behind our house," Rosie said. "They would yell, 'Hey, nigger!' So my older brothers and sisters would yell back, 'Hey peckerwoods!' This worried my mother. 'Don't you call them that!' she scolded. 'It isn't right!' She was real scared they would stop and beat us up or any of a number of other things. She didn't want us to be known among whites as 'troublemakers.'"

After Rosie finished, I told some of my own mother's stories about white terror, and about the time when she was put in jail for no reason. I also told how my sister and I confronted the landlord who tried to cheat us when we were sharecropping. "That was a victory of sorts for us," I remarked, "to get what we knew we had coming to us. But we paid the price—no more sharecropping!" They all understood.

As we talked about problems, we realized that we were a new generation, and that times were changing. Our mothers and fathers and their generation had dealt with racial issues passively, by giving way to whites and not bucking the system. But we were all convinced that it was time to work for change in the system. Yet we wanted to press for change in a nonviolent way, like Martin Luther King and others had been doing. We also wanted to act from a biblical basis, the way Brother Perkins was doing. We all liked the way that he was concerned about housing and food and justice and education as well as pointing people toward Christ.

It didn't take long for us to start working on Rosie to apply to LABC, especially now that Carolyn had been accepted. She admitted that the idea of going to a Christian college appealed to her. "But I already have a scholarship to Alcorn State University," she explained. "Besides, how am I going to pay for it? I planned to do farm work this summer to earn money for my expenses. But now that I've stayed here, I'm not sure what I'm going to do."

We assured her that if God wanted her at LABC, He'd provide the finances. So we started praying that everything would work out. One day she announced her decision to apply: "God has led me this far, and He will see me through." This was remarkably strong faith for a new Christian.

She knew that if she was accepted, she'd be among the first black female students. I also had warned her that classes would be hard. "When you consider the time you lost doing farm work during school years, you'll be entering college with about three years less school time than your white classmates!" I told her. But she'd made up her mind that God would help her.

Several weeks later she received her letter of acceptance as a freshman. By the time fall arrived, we'd brought the number of blacks at LABC up to seven. That helped improve campus life for us quite a bit. When there had been only two of us, the white majority could more easily avoid having to deal with us. But seven—that was a definite presence, enough to fill a table in the cafeteria or sit as a group in chapel. We discovered that we could use our numbers to shake up the status quo!

On one occasion, for instance, a man from Bob Jones University spoke in chapel. Bob Jones was a school with a reputation for discriminating against blacks. So all seven of us sat together right in the front row, just to make sure he knew we were there. I think he found it unsettling. Some of the white kids thought it was funny, and they understood what we were trying to do. Others got a little upset.

One distinct advantage of having female black students on campus was that it gave me a chance to date! A few weeks into the semester I asked Rosie out. As we talked about her experience in this new place, I detected some discomfort about college. "You seem to be under a lot of tension," I remarked.

"I guess so," she answered. "I've never been around white people before, except to pick cotton or do a little work for them. Here the whole town is white. Almost everyone in my classes is white. Even my roommate is white."

"Is she prejudiced?"

"Not particularly. She hasn't given me any reason to think so. Oh, we have a few problems, like when to turn out the light if one of us wants to sleep and the other one study. Nothing big. But the problem is, I can't seem to talk about these little problems with her. I mean, I've never spoken up to a white person!"

Like so many blacks, Rosie had been conditioned to "know her place" with whites. Even though she was now in an atmosphere that permitted her to speak up or disagree with her white roommate, she couldn't. Externally, she was free to speak her mind, but internally she was still bound by the fear of being considered "rebellious."

In Mississippi, a black was regarded as rebellious if she dared even to look a white person in the eye. The "proper" way was to talk with her head down, looking away. That showed the proper "respect" toward the white person. Even today, if you're

66

white or if you're a black who has attained a lot of status and success, you can find blacks who are still so damaged that they won't look you in the eye. They'll look every place else, but not in your eye.

That was the system. It trained blacks to act like inferiors. And when you act inferior long enough, and have your inferiority reinforced often enough, you start to think of yourself as inferior.

My mother, for example, baby-sat for a white boy who lived nearby. Ironically, the man who moved his fence onto our property and stole our land was this boy's father. But Mama cared for that boy all the time he was growing up, feeding him, washing him, scolding him. Then when he turned nineteen and became an adult member of the white community, she had to start acting inferior, calling him "Mister so-and-so" and answering him yes sir and no sir. To do otherwise would have been "rebellious."

This situation was why Rosie had a hard time trying to deal with simple, common disagreements with her roommate. Every time she felt like standing up for herself or imposing on her roommate, a little voice seemed to remind her, "Don't be rebellious!"

Rosie was struggling with other issues besides hassles with her roommate. She wasn't making ends meet financially. She'd pieced together as much financial aid as she could between a small scholarship, a loan, and a work-study program in the library.

"But it's still not enough," she told me. "I'm getting notes from the business office because I'm behind in my bill. I have nowhere to go for money, so I just pray about it." I marveled at her trust in God. I was even more amazed, though, when I found out that she had left Mississippi for California with only nine dollars in her pocket! She was so committed to getting an education at LABC and so convinced that God wanted her there that she had come all the way out there assuming that God would somehow provide. It gave a whole new meaning to what she had said back in Mendenhall about trusting God to see her through!

Rosie wasn't the only black student struggling financially. Several of the others were hurting, too. Jimmie and I had the advantage of basketball scholarships. But the others were on their own to pay the costs of attending a private Christian college. Unless help arrived soon, some of the kids might have to drop out.

One night the president of the college requested a meeting with all the black students. We all showed up at his office, not knowing what to expect. He introduced us to two white women—Betty Wagner and Muriel Hamlin. They were from Samaritan's Purse, an organization set up to help people with financial needs. They had learned that some of the black students were having financial problems, so they came to tell us that any bills we couldn't pay would be taken care of.

You could just feel everyone's tension relax when they said that! It was a miracle. "This lets me know for sure that God really wants me here!" Rosie exclaimed as we left the president's office. We all realized that a lot of prayers had just been answered.

Another answer to prayer was my graduation from LABC in the spring. God had fulfilled Jimmie's and my dream of (and commitment to) being racial pioneers, the first two blacks to ever graduate from all-white Los Angeles Baptist College. I was bursting with pride as I walked across the stage, shook hands with the president, and received my diploma. In my mind I could see all the people along the way who hadn't wanted me to get that far. Some had never even wanted me to get out of Mississippi. Now I had triumphed. I kept thinking, *Man, I've made it!*

Best of all, my mother was in the crowd, surrounded by the most whites she'd ever seen at one time. But everyone treated her with great respect and congratulations. The trip to California and the commencement was a highlight in her life. I think she knew, more than anyone else, what graduating from LABC meant for me.

As for my immediate future, I'd already been accepted at Los Angeles Baptist Theological Seminary and would also coach the freshman basketball team at LABC. However, I returned to Mendenhall for the summer. This time, as we evaluated the needs of children in Simpson County, we realized that many were getting ready to go into a newly integrated school system. Having come from grossly inferior schools, we knew that they would be behind from the start. We knew that many would grow discouraged and eventually drop out.

So we decided to start a tutorial program to get them as ready as possible for the new situation. We also realized that we could use this program as an opportunity to train some young leaders in the Mendenhall community. We recruited eight or ten young people and prepared them to tutor the kids.

A related bit of excitement was that two white college students, Chris Herb and Nancy Fox, came from the North to help us. Chris proved invaluable in organizing the tutorial program and training the tutors. The presence of these two women was a breakthrough of sorts in Mendenhall. They were the first whites to work with the black community as volunteers.

Back in California in the fall, I continued to date Rosie, now in her second year at LABC. By the end of September, I'd made up my mind: I was going to ask her to marry me. The date I picked for the special moment was February 26—her birthday. If she said yes to my proposal, I hoped to marry her on August 7—*my* birthday!

So I went to a store in the area and picked out a ring. I was just making nickels at the time, barely scraping by. But somehow I managed to start paying money down on the ring every month. I hoped to pay it off by the end of February.

Then in early November I got a call from Overseas Crusades, the mission organization. "Dolphus, we're thinking of organizing a basketball team to tour the Orient this summer as a mission outreach. If we do it, would you consider being a part?"

The idea turned my engagement plans completely upside down. Sure, I wanted to travel overseas! But in the summer? That would wreck my plans for an August 7 wedding. Still, I decided that a trip like that would be a once-in-a-lifetime experience. So I decided that I'd rearrange my plans. I told Overseas Crusades to count on me, and they said they'd let me know once they got things organized.

Well, I didn't hear anything the rest of November. December came—still no word. I kept paying down on the ring. When January slipped away with still no confirmation, I figured that the trip was off. So I began to finalize my plans to propose to Rosie.

On February 26 I went to the jewelry store and made my final payment on the engagement ring. Then I stopped for flowers, a box of candy, and a card to give her. I planned to take her out to dinner that evening and propose then, so I asked around to locate a restaurant worthy of the occasion. I settled on one aboard a ship docked along the coast. Reservations made, I hurried back to campus, hoping to catch Rosie at the dorm before she left for class.

"Happy Birthday, Rosie!" I exclaimed as I handed her the candy, flowers, and card. I'd already asked her out to dinner, so I said, "See you at seven!" and hurried off to my own classes—with the little square box deep in my pocket!

It was sort of a waste of time attending class that day. All I could think about was dinner that night. What if she said no? The question hadn't occurred to me before I bought the ring. Now it caused me considerable anxiety. Maybe I should have asked her before I bought the ring! As classes dragged on, I felt more and more uneasy.

At last I finished the day, got ready, picked her up, and we were on our way to the restaurant in Santa Monica. While we ate I managed to keep up my end of the conversation. But The Question was constantly on my mind. Finally the time seemed right. So I asked her point-blank: "Rosie, will you marry me?"

She didn't answer immediately, which scared me. And when she finally did, it wasn't what I'd expected. "Dolphus, let's pray first." And so we prayed, right there in the floating restaurant on the coast.

When we finished, I waited expectantly for her answer. Finally she said, "Yes, Dolphus! I believe you're the one God wants me to marry." Then she went on to explain, "I really wasn't thinking about marriage right now. I was making my own plans. You know, I never wanted to be the usual black role model like a teacher, or a maid, or a housewife. I wanted to be something different—like a model. But at the same time I've been praying—even before I dated you—that God would show me when the right man for me came along. So when you asked me just now, I needed to know if you were the one."

"How did you decide?"

"During the prayer, my doubts went away. God gave me peace."

I smiled as I reached into my coat pocket, brought out the little box, and slipped the ring on her finger.

The next day I got a letter from Overseas Crusades. The tour was on! And they wanted me to be a part. The good news was that the dates for travel were May 2 through June 20, so the trip would have no bearing on our wedding plans. The bad news was that each player would have to raise his own fifteen-hundred-dollar airfare. So I figured that was the end of that. No way could I raise that kind of money—not by May!

But in the days that followed I didn't have much time to think about money or the tour or Overseas Crusades. Nor did I have time to think about my upcoming wedding. Something else gripped my attention: back in Mississippi John Perkins was fighting for his life.

E I G H T

DO THE MEN

THAT BEAT US

WORSHIP THE SAME GOD?

"Dolphus, pray for John! Get as many students as you can and pray to God because he's in jail, and they're going to kill him!" John Perkins's wife, Vera, was on the phone. I could feel the terror and urgency in her voice.

I knew what she said was true: If Mississippi whites were holding him, anything could happen—beating, torture, even murder. I felt so helpless, since there was nothing I could do—except pray.

I remembered the night Martin Luther King died, how alone I'd felt, listening to the students down the hall laughing and cheering. Would I get a similar response this time? I could just hear the skepticism with which white students would respond to an appeal from a black kid for prayer for a stranger in jail in Mississippi. "In jail? What was he doing wrong? Was he breaking the law with all this civil rights stuff and demonstrations? Hey, this is America—they don't put you in jail if you're obeying the law! He must be a troublemaker!"

But I realized I was wasting time in such speculations. Vera had asked me to gather everyone I could and have prayer. I told her I would. I needed to just trust God and do it. So I went around to different guys in my dorm and asked them to meet in my room for a prayer meeting. I also called Rosie to ask her to organize something over at LABC. Soon a small group had gathered, and we prayed for a while, calling on God to protect John and comfort Vera.

When we finished, everyone had lots of questions about what was going on. So I began to explain who John Perkins was and what he was trying to accomplish through Voice of Calvary. I found the group to be genuinely interested and realized I had a great opportunity to tell them what life was like for blacks in Mississippi.

Eventually I got around to why I thought John had been put in jail. A few weeks before, I had been home for Christmas, and things had been real tense between blacks and whites. Roy Berry, Carolyn Albritton's cousin, had been accused of phoning a white woman, so the authorities put him in jail, and while he was there they beat him so badly that we thought he wasn't going to live. The incident not only outraged the black community, it also made us afraid of what might happen to anyone else who was arrested.

Things heated up the next day when a young black man named Garland Wilks got into an argument with a white store-owner in Mendenhall. Apparently he'd been "rebellious," raising his voice to the man and standing his ground instead of giving him the usual yes sir and no sir and leaving the store when told to.

By coincidence, John Perkins was in the store when this incident occurred. Knowing what would happen if Garland got arrested, John stepped in and convinced him to leave before there was trouble. In fact, just to make sure that there wouldn't be any more trouble, John offered to give Garland a ride home.

The store owner, however, was pretty upset and called the police. Before John could get the fellow home, the police stopped his car and arrested Garland. They let John go, and he returned to the ministry's headquarters. Soon the news was all over black Mendenhall that another arrest had been made, and everyone figured that meant another beating—or worse. Garland's grandmother showed up to talk to John and sank in despair. "They've taken Garland," she moaned, "and they're going to beat him tonight! I just know they're going to beat him!"

Finally John decided that the best thing to do was to go up to the jail and keep an eye on things. Since Roy Berry was still there, Carolyn asked to go, and so did Doug Huemmer, a white man who had been helping out in the ministry. John's four kids also wanted to go. And about that time a group of kids rehearsing a Christmas program let out, so ten more children went along.

So John and this big group of people, mostly kids, and one white man showed up at the Mendenhall jail. That must have startled the jailer! When John started asking questions about Garland and Roy, the jailer told them, "Go on! Get out of here!" They argued back and forth for a while until the jailer finally put the whole lot of them in jail—including the children.

Vera and I were called to come up to the jail. Before we left we contacted a lot of people, who in turn contacted more people. Before long, dozens of blacks, including nearly all the leaders of black Mendenhall, were crossing the railroad tracks and marching up Main Street to the jail. About forty or fifty of us sat down and held a vigil outside the building, hoping that our presence might deter any violence on the inside. We really were afraid that the police were going to beat John for daring to come see Garland and Roy.

But as the night wore on and we discussed the situation, I could tell that there was also a potential for violence on the part of blacks. Some people seemed willing to do anything to get themselves arrested so as to pack the jail and embarrass the authorities. Some of us counseled peace and nonviolence. "Let's not do anything irrational," we said. "That won't solve anything."

Still, we all felt something had to be done. Somehow we had to let the white community know that we weren't going to put up with beatings and false arrests and illegal searches, to say nothing of the overall climate of injustice in the system. We wanted to see blacks on the police force and in other government jobs. We wanted the minimum wage law applied fairly to us. We wanted our streets paved and wanted our kids to be able to use the parks and pools.

We wondered what kind of strategy we could devise to press for these kinds of changes. Complaining about a jailer who had locked up a few black children in jail wouldn't do any good. Nor would we get anywhere if our leaders all got arrested. We had to do something that would get white folks' attention without causing more violence.

Not surprisingly, the person who came up with the best suggestion was John Perkins. All through the night he had called out to us from inside the jail, letting us know what was happening. He also preached to us, trying to defuse the tension. In a way, he was as much a part of our discussion that night as anyone, even though he wasn't among us there in the crowd. His idea was to stage a boycott of white businesses in town.

The suggestion was immediately adopted. Right away we began to spread the word: "Don't shop in Mendenhall!" By the time the police released John the next evening, every black person in town knew about it.

As a part of our strategy we also organized marches, with signs and songs to demonstrate our grievances. The white authorities took careful note of our activities. As we marched around town, the highway patrol stood by, armed with tear gas, billy clubs, and shotguns. Technically, by Mississippi's outdated laws of segregation, we were committing a crime by advocating equality between the races!

But the boycott and the marches went on, long after the other West Coast students and I had returned to school. Students from Tougaloo College, a black school in Jackson, took our places.

One Saturday after the march, Doug Huemmer was driving a van with nineteen kids back to Tougaloo. Suddenly a highway patrolman pulled Doug over and arrested the entire group. Later the charges were revealed: "Reckless driving and carrying in the van a concealed deadly brick." He and fellow officers took them up to Brandon and put them in jail. Brandon was another town known for beating blacks. Its sheriff had abused both black and white civil rights workers trying to register people to vote.

When John Perkins heard about the arrests, he went to post bail for Doug and the others. Vera grew worried when he didn't come home and she didn't hear from him. Then an anonymous phone caller terrorized her by asking, "Have they hung them yet?"

That's when she called me and the prayer meeting began. As I related all of this to my fellow seminarians, they began to see that life for black people in Mississippi was worse than they realized. They prayed with me late into the night.

As we prayed, I kept reflecting on Paul's brave words to Timothy: "Remember that Jesus Christ, of the seed of David, was raised from the dead according to my gospel, for which I suffer trouble as an evildoer, even to the point of chains; but the word of God is not chained" (2 Timothy 2:8-9).

Near morning I lay in bed, exhausted but unable to sleep. I was thinking back to the killing of Martin Luther King and beyond that to the assassination of John F. Kennedy. Both those men had done so much to help blacks. Why did they have to get cut down, just when good things had started to happen?

My real question had to do with God's justice: Why did He let the people who were looking out for our concerns get killed, while He let the people with their feet on our necks keep on living? It just didn't seem right. I was angry—angry at God!

I didn't resolve the issue that night. In some ways I still haven't—except I'm convinced that God is just. I also realize that I don't have the whole picture, as God does. So I trust that He knows what He's doing, even if I don't understand it. Someday He'll make it plain to me and set things right. But for now it's enough for me to accept that He is just.

After a sleepless night, I dressed and went to classes. But my heart and mind weren't in the material. Finally that night, word came. I dreaded what I might hear. I knew God was able to protect John in any situation—just as He'd been able to protect Dr. King and President Kennedy. But would He? Or would He choose to accomplish His purposes by letting John die—just as He had with the others? I didn't think I could handle it if I heard that it had happened again. So when I learned that John was still alive—even though he'd been beaten and tortured—I broke down and thanked God for His intervention.

Later I learned about how he'd been treated in jail. "This is the smart nigger," the Brandon police had sneered when John arrived at the jail to post bail for Doug and the students. They knew John from photographs taken by the authorities during the marches in Mendenhall. Once in the jail, he was stomped and kicked in the head, ribs, and groin until he lay on the floor in a tight ball, trying to protect himself. Five policemen at a time beat him unconscious with blackjacks and billy clubs. A man named Curry Brown had come with John, and he was arrested also. He and Doug were slapped, punched, and kicked while they were handcuffed. They were accused of being communist agitators. Their heads were shaved, and moonshine was poured on their wounds.

At one point someone said that the FBI was coming, so the sheriff forced John, who by then could barely stand, to mop up all the blood. The FBI never came, and before long the beatings resumed. While they tormented John, they forced him to read a written list of demands that had been printed up for the boycott. At one point they held an unloaded gun to his head and pulled the trigger. After all of this, he was again beaten bloody until he lost consciousness.

Even the Tougaloo College students were beaten. When one student demanded that the sheriff respect his constitutional rights, the sheriff jeered at him, "Nigger, I'm going to give you your constitutional rights, your marching rights, and your civil rights!" Then he kicked the young man while the others joined in and beat him with blackjacks and billy clubs.

Later John told me, "They were like savages. At one point they took a fork and bent down the two middle prongs. Then they pushed the other two up my nose until blood spurted out."

Meanwhile, Vera and others had arrived at the Brandon jail to try to get release of their family members. But they were told that they'd first have to raise bail money. Nathan Rubin, the president of the Simpson County Civic League, drove all over Rankin County that night trying to find black folks with enough property to cover bond for the twenty-three people in jail.

A few days later, John was tried by a justice of the peace for the December 23 incident in Mendenhall. Neither he nor his lawyer was told what the charge was. But he was found guilty and sentenced to three months in jail, plus a thirty-three-dollar fine. When John appealed the case in circuit court, the charge was finally named: contributing to the delinquency of a minor.

I was sure that this was a calculated move to undermine John's effectiveness as a youth leader. What better way to silence a preacher than to call him a corrupter of children? The authorities accused him of encouraging the children to stay in jail that night. But somehow the jailer forgot to mention that he was the one who had locked the door behind them! In the trial, Georgia Ann Quinn, the eleven-year-old, testified that

Reverend Perkins had never asked her to come to the jail in the first place; that was her own idea. Besides, her behavior had never been delinquent in any way.

Nevertheless, John was found guilty. On appeal to the state supreme court, a deal was worked out: John would admit to disturbing the peace and the county would drop the delinquency charge. It wasn't the justice we would have hoped for. But a number of powerful moral victories came out of the decision. We all saw a black man stand up to the system, and we watched a young black female lawyer, Constance Slaughter, keep John out of jail.

The outcome also sent a message to the lower, local courts and to the police and sheriffs that things were going to have to start changing. The days were over when they could treat blacks like animals. More than anything else, the black community united as never before. For months no blacks shopped in Mendenhall.

The Brandon beatings took much longer to resolve in court. Again there was some horse-trading involved: John had to drop his charges of police brutality in exchange for the reckless driving and concealed deadly brick charges against Doug and the students. No one involved in the beatings was ever punished. But again there were important moral victories won by the black community. At last the plight of blacks and their mistreatment in Mississippi was gaining the attention of leaders in the white community. Chief Justice of the U.S. Court of Appeals John R. Brown wrote in his opinion of *Perkins v. State of Mississippi* (p. 12):

> The record is replete with uncontested evidence of patently frivolous arrests for nonexistent offenses, threatened and actual physical violence, almost unbelievably humiliating and degrading treatment . . . that far surpasses the official brutality we have only recently condemned as cruel and unusual punishment violating the Eighth Amendment. . . . There is literally no evidence to support any of the charges against the 23 defendants.

John and the others from Mendenhall were not alone in their struggles with the system. That spring was a difficult time

for black people all over Mississippi. By April, black community centers in West Point and Flora and seven black churches
in Washington, Pinola, and Leake Counties had been burned.
In May, carloads of young whites drove through the Jackson
State University campus, shouting racial insults and throwing
beer cans. Black students countered by throwing rocks. Soon a
full-scale riot was underway. But instead of using tear gas, the
seventy-five highway patrolmen assigned to quell the distur-
bance fired four hundred rounds of ammunition into a crowd
of a hundred black students and through three floors of a
women's dorm. Two students were killed and several were
injured. This was how Mississippi "controlled" black students.

As reports of these incidents reached California, I was
amazed at how they were interpreted, especially among
whites. The skepticism that I'd feared surfaced, especially at
some of the churches that had helped John get started with
Voice of Calvary. Since I was something of a representative for
the ministry, they asked me, "Is Voice of Calvary involved in
any of the civil rights movement? They were suspicious of the
movement as a whole, and hearing about violence in Mississippi, such that troops had to be called out, didn't help. Nor did
they like hearing that John was registering voters and leading
boycotts.

When I tried to explain what was happening back home, I
was told flatly, "We don't think you need to be involved in the
civil rights movement." They didn't understand. They were
linking their continued support to our willingness to disasso-
ciate ourselves from the struggle for equality. Finally I replied,
"Do you believe that God can give us discernment about the
kinds of things we get involved in? If so, then trust Him—and
trust us. But if not, maybe it would be best not to support John
and Voice of Calvary."

A number of churches did cut off their support. As a result,
funds for the ministry grew very tight. This only added to the
pressures John was under, and I wasn't surprised when his
health broke down. He had a severe ulcer and part of his
stomach had to be removed.

The behavior of whites in Mississippi and the attitude of
whites in California mystified me. Both claimed to worship and
serve the same God I did. Yet many of the whites there in

southern California seemed to believe that black Christians could choose Jesus Christ or civil rights—but not both. And in Mississippi, white men would beat blacks on Saturday night yet sit in church and claim to worship God on Sunday morning.

It made no sense. In fact, at that point only one thing made much sense to me: I'd made it out of the terrible system in Mississippi, and I had no intention of ever going back.

NINE

BACK HOME

TO MISSISSIPPI . . .

AS GOD WISHES

If I had one ticket out of Mississippi, it was basketball. Not that I ever had NBA potential. But basketball had gotten me a scholarship to Piney Woods Junior College, then another to LABC. Then, by coaching that school's freshman basketball team, I was able to pay my first and second year tuition at Los Angeles Baptist Theological Seminary.

Basketball was also responsible for forcing me to decide what I was going to do after seminary—in effect, what I was going to do with my life.

I've already described how Overseas Crusades sent me an invitation to tour the Orient with its basketball team, the Crusaders. But given the fifteen-hundred-dollar airfare I'd have to raise, I figured it was out of my league.

Then along came Larry Bassinet and Cal Luening of Osborne Neighborhood Church. They invited me to tell their congregation about the proposed trip, and when my speech raised over $300, I took heart. Maybe I could raise the money after all, with God's help. So I began to visit churches on Sunday mornings, along with Norm Cook, the coach. When people began to give me ten dollars here and fifteen there, I realized that God wanted me to go on that tour.

Finally, just days before my deadline for raising the money, a church member in Menlo Park asked me, "How much do you still need?"

"About four hundred," I answered, wishing it were less. He wrote out a check for two hundred dollars. Another member gave a hundred and fifty, and the collection plate brought in the rest. I was astounded that people believed so much in what our team was doing. I was also humbled that they would believe in me personally.

A few days later I sat in a jet high above the Pacific. I wondered, *What am I doing here? I'm just a poor boy from Mississippi, yet here I am on my way to the Orient! Who would have believed it!*

But even more powerful than my excitement over traveling overseas was my excitement for our mission. I felt so privileged to be a part of an effort to preach the gospel. With all of the crises in Mississippi during the previous year and the focus on the civil rights movement sweeping across America, so many people around me had assumed that I was more concerned with racial equality and social justice than with the spiritual condition of people. But that wasn't so.

In fact, all along my heartbeat had been for evangelism. It still is because even if a person enjoys the freedom of his rights under the law, he still needs freedom from sin, and only Jesus Christ can give him that. Furthermore, racism itself is deeply rooted in sin. So the ultimate answer to racism is to bring people into a relationship with Christ, so that He can begin to overcome the hatred and bigotry that binds them.

As I mentioned earlier, some of the churches in California that had been supporting John Perkins saw a dichotomy between social justice and evangelism: either John was preaching civil rights or he was preaching the gospel. Somehow they couldn't see that these were not opposites. It was not either/or, but both/and.

I guess they were afraid that if John and Voice of Calvary concerned themselves with justice issues, he might lose sight of preaching the gospel. But as someone who had grown up in the underclass of Simpson County and knew all too well how destructive the system of segregation there could be, I looked at things just the opposite: How could someone preach the gospel and not be concerned with what it means for racism? I had great respect for John because he saw the important connection between these two.

I wanted to tell people about Jesus, too. And so, as our plane soared over the water below, I felt a tremendous sense of purpose in what I was doing. I was not just on a vacation, using basketball to sightsee my way across the Orient. I was going as an ambassador of Jesus Christ to people who had probably never heard the gospel story.

As soon as we landed we went right to work, playing three games a day, then traveling many miles between games. As the only black on the team, I felt a little uncomfortable, especially because some of the players came from colleges and seminaries where black students were not accepted. But as we began to function as a team, things loosened up. With so much time on the road together, we got into some great discussions, and I think a lot of barriers were broken down and trust established.

The rigorous schedule was tiring, but my enthusiasm was unbounded, especially when our fans responded so well. I mentioned a few of their comments earlier. What began to amaze me was how much they responded to me in particular. "They win the competition not roughly, but skillfully and politely, especially #14 Mr. Weary," one Chinese wrote. Another said, "After the play was over, I went up to the hall in order to listen to their preaching and singing. Mr. Weary, who is a negro, acted as a chairman this morning. He told us about their purposes of coming. This has a great effect on me for I am not a good Christian as they are. They are good examples to me and I hope that through the power of Jesus I can became a good and obedient Christian."

This kind of response was new to me. I'd shared my testimony back home and in California and seen people respond to my presentation of the gospel. But never like this! I began to feel a new sense of my own worth as a person. It was as if God had taken me to the other side of the world to show me the value that I had.

So when Norm asked me to consider making a career out of preaching the gospel to Asians, I thought that I'd finally found my mission in life. Here was something positive, a ministry that people seemed to welcome. Wherever we went, smiling faces greeted us. People clapped and cheered. They crowded around to hear our words. And many responded to our invitations to accept Christ as their Savior.

Best of all, this work was half a world away from Mississippi. All my life I'd wanted out. Now I'd made it out, and I could stay out. I could stay as far away from Mississippi as a person could get! Away from white folks who thought that because I was black they could lie to me and cheat me and steal from me. Away from authorities like the animals who had beaten John Perkins. Away from a system where I was a second-class citizen, without rights, without dignity, without hope.

That was the shame of Mississippi—it offered no hope to me or any other black person. Those who could left. Those who stayed learned to live invisibly, to escape notice by the whites, to avoid trouble. It was better to leave. I'd left. Here was a chance to stay out.

Norm proposed his idea early in the trip. It was a smart recruiting move because things got better and better during the next six weeks. After more than sixty ball games, I was as confident in front of the crowds as if I'd been doing it for a lifetime. The team was operating as a unit. And we all felt that the tour had exceeded our expectations.

And during that six weeks God was speaking to me—only He wasn't telling me to give my life to the Far East. Incredibly, He seemed to be telling me to go back home instead, back to Simpson County, back to the pain and problems there. There was no dramatic turning point when I made my decision. It was just a conversation that went on for six weeks. Gradually a conviction grew inside me that God wanted me in Mississippi.

Of course, I gave Him plenty of reasons why not! For one thing, I knew Rosie would never agree to it. Like me, she wanted a life away from the ugliness of a racially segregated system. She'd want a family, and she'd never raise children in the same place where she'd experienced so much bigotry.

Rosie . . . I missed her so much! What was it she had told me before I left for the trip? It was a Scripture passage, Psalm 91! She'd told me to keep reading Psalm 91, with its great message of hope and protection (verses 1-4):

> He who dwells in the secret place of the Most High
> Shall abide under the shadow of the Almighty.
> I will say of the LORD,
> "He is my refuge and my fortress;

My God, in Him I will trust."
Surely He shall deliver you from the snare of the fowler
And from the perilous pestilence.
He shall cover you with His feathers,
And under His wings you shall take refuge;
His truth shall be your shield and buckler.

I read those verses night after night on my bunk after we'd finished our games. The more I pondered them, the more I saw Mississippi. If ever there was a place where a man needed to take refuge in God, it was there! I thought of the terrors that lay in wait for black people, the kind of uncertainty that my grand-mother's suitor had voiced: "I'll see you next week—if I be livin!" But the psalm offered the comfort (v. 5-10):

You shall not be afraid of the terror by night,
Nor of the arrow that flies by day,
Nor of the pestilence that walks in darkness,
Nor of the destruction that lays waste at noonday.
A thousand may fall at your side,
And ten thousand at your right hand;
But it shall not come near you.
Only with your eyes shall you look,
And see the reward of the wicked.
Because you have made the LORD, who is my refuge,
Even the Most High, your habitation,
No evil shall befall you,
Nor shall any plague come near your dwelling.

I thought long and hard about God's compassion for people. Every day I saw His concern for the people in the Far East, so many of whom lived in conditions worse than the ones I'd grown up in. And I also knew He felt compassion for the folks back home. I'd seen that compassion displayed through John and his helpers. God cared about the injustice, the poverty, the hopelessness.

But one day I realized something else: God cared about *me*. "Dolphus," He seemed to say to me one night, "you're black and I love you. You were born in the South, and I love you. You ought not to run away from your blackness or the fact that you're from the South. Don't you know that in Me you have security?"

Then I realized that in seeking to stay in Taiwan, I was really running away *from* something, not *toward* something. I was running away from Mendenhall, from all that Mendenhall represented. Only I realized that no matter how far I ran, whether to California or even to Taiwan, I could never run away from the Mendenhall inside of me, the one in my head and in my heart. Until I overcame that, I'd always be enslaved to a sense of hopelessness. And yet I knew that in myself I couldn't overcome it—only God could. Only He could give me a hope, not just for a better house or a better car or a better life—but hope for becoming the person He'd created me to be.

Seen from this angle, the prospect of giving my life to the ministry in Taiwan began to seem selfish. I knew there was nothing wrong with enjoying the people there and basking in their enthusiastic response. But my main motivation for it would be selfish; I'd be doing it more because of what it would do for me than what it would do for them.

By contrast, going back to Mississippi seemed to involve service and a sacrifice of my own desires on behalf of others who needed hope. I felt that God was urging me, "Dolphus, I have something for you to do in Mississippi."

But I felt weighed down thinking about coming back to the South, especially to my hometown. I staggered at how difficult it would be to motivate people there to see that change is possible—especially when so many felt as I had always felt: "There's nothing you can do! The situation will never change! It's hopeless!" One comfort was the promise of God in Psalm 91:14-16:

> Because he has set his love upon Me, therefore I will deliver him;
> I will set him on high, because he has known My name.
> He shall call upon Me, and I will answer him;
> I will be with him in trouble; I will deliver him and honor him.
> With long life I will satisfy him,
> And show him My salvation.

The decision to return to Mendenhall was six weeks in the making. I don't know when I crossed the line. I just remember that when I came back from the trip, the question was not whether I would return, but when.

First I had to finish seminary. But before that, I had something even more important to fulfill: my wedding to Rosie on August 15. We traveled back to Mississippi for it. The service took place at New Zion Baptist Church, and then everyone came back to Mendenhall for the reception.

In the fall we headed back to Los Angeles for my final year in seminary and Rosie's junior year at LABC. She continued to work in the college library, and I continued coaching. Now we had two paychecks coming in, for a total income of two hundred dollars a month. Our only debt was a sixty-one-dollar payment on a VW Beetle. So we felt rich! We had more money than either of us had ever seen. In fact, it was tempting to think about what could happen once I added a master's degree in Christian education to my undergraduate degree from LABC. The life-style in California looked incredibly appealing to two young people who had had so little for so long.

But even though we fantasized about settling down in California, we never really considered it as a serious option. What God had been saying to me in Taiwan, He was still saying to me in California. I had told Rosie before we were married that I was feeling like He wanted me to go back to Mendenhall. She hadn't been too enthusiastic!

"Dolphus, you and I dreamed about getting away from Mississippi. We said we'd never go back. Things are no better now. Look what John's been through this year! His family threatened, his health is ruined! Besides, I don't believe God opened all these doors for me to go to college just to send me back to Mendenhall."

I didn't blame her one bit for feeling as she did. I'd always felt the same. But I also knew that she would pray about it. So I asked God to help her in whatever way she needed.

Several days later she brought up the subject. "Dolphus, I guess this is the first time in my life I've ever faced a conflict between what I wanted and what God apparently wants for me. Up to now He's pretty much allowed me to pursue the wishes of my heart. So I was angry when you told me you felt God was leading you back to Mississippi. I felt I was going to get cheated out of my dream for a better life. But when I told my friends how I felt, they asked me if I was truly looking for God's will. You know, I had to tell them I hadn't even prayed about it! I was so upset. All I could think of was my disappointment."

She paused, and I wondered what she was leading up to.

"I've prayed about it a lot since then. And I've decided that I'm going to go where my husband's heart is. I have to tell you, I don't feel the same call, so I'll go reluctantly. But if God is calling you to a great work, I think He's calling me to an equally great work—being your wife!"

When I heard that, my heart soared! But one thing I didn't want was for the return to Mendenhall to keep her from finishing college. So we decided that during the summer she could take classes at Jackson State College, about a half-hour's drive from Mendenhall. Then in the fall she could return to LABC to take the few remaining hours she needed to get her degree.

In the spring of 1971, I did what I swore I'd never do: I moved with my new bride back to Mississippi, back to where it all began. There was little to cheer about. John Perkins had moved up to Jackson. The only programs operating were after-school tutoring and a radio ministry. The gains of the civil rights movement were trickling down slowly to rural areas like Simpson County. And whatever funds would be needed had yet to be raised, starting from scratch.

Was this really where God wanted me? I thought back to the tour in the Orient. "Dolphus, I have something for you to do in Mississippi." What was it? I looked around. Were these children playing in the streets really so different from the children on the streets in Hong Kong? Were these women holding families together through backbreaking work and iron-strong willpower any different from the mothers I'd seen in the Philippines? Were the men I saw in the evenings gathered on the porches any different from the men in the hamlets of Taiwan?

If God could use me to speak to people in the Far East, certainly He could use me to help people in my own hometown. But I saw right away that *He* would have to make it happen. From a human standpoint, it looked hopeless; certainly it seemed beyond my abilities. But this time as I looked at the situation, I didn't despair. I believed God was with me, and was saying to me what He'd said to David in Psalm 91:16: "Behold My salvation!"

TEN

CHANGING AN

UNCHANGEABLE SYSTEM

When I came home to Mendenhall in 1971, I had very little idea about what I was supposed to do. All I knew was that I wanted to address the needs of poor people and somehow create an oasis of hope in a low-income community. Actually, I had envisioned some sort of partnership with John Perkins. He had already laid a foundation through his work in Mendenhall and his activism on behalf of blacks. So I cast him as the visionary, the fund-raiser, the person out generating interest in whatever it was we would be doing. Meanwhile, I would be the one on the scene as a director, administrator, and manager.

But things didn't quite work out that way. By the time Rosie and I arrived, John had relocated thirty miles north to Jackson. The Perkins family had gone through a terrible year. John had suffered a heart attack in addition to having ulcer surgery after his jailing in Mendenhall and the beatings in Brandon. Meanwhile, his cases crept through the court system, where only a minority opinion from Judge Brown of the Mississippi State Supreme Court gave him any hope that a flicker of justice existed in the system. When he lost his appeal, bomb threats and other violence by the Ku Klux Klan mounted. Finally, the pressure on his family became unbearable. So they left for Jackson. He and Vera Mae commuted down each day. But it was clear that his ministry in Mendenhall was coming to a close.

So I began to pray about what was needed in Mendenhall. What sorts of chronic problems needed to be solved? And what would it take to solve them? The vision that began to take shape during the rest of that year and the next two was how we could create some of the same opportunities and advantages in black Mendenhall that existed in more affluent communities. What struck me about our town was the established belief that because blacks here lived without things like decent health care or affordable legal services, they always would. There was an assumption that that was the way things were, and they would never change.

But what needed to change was that way of thinking because it trapped people into cycles of poverty. Moreover, it trapped them psychologically, so that even if opportunities came along, they wouldn't be able to make use of them.

The question was, Where to begin? The logical choice was to focus on youth. They were malleable. Many of the people over forty had been severely damaged by the system. They had spent so many years as second-class citizens that trying to change their minds would take extraordinary energy and a lot of time. We felt more hopeful about the young people.

One of the things I wanted most was to see them continue their schooling and learn skills that would lead to better jobs. Instead, most were dropping out. There were several reasons. First, they were way behind to begin with. When Mississippi integrated its schools in the early 1970s, a lot of blacks couldn't compete against white children who had had better schools. The black students had been attending segregated schools where the quality of instruction and materials was often poor. And they'd also missed too many days picking cotton and doing other farm chores. To make matters worse, many of their parents didn't encourage them to do well. They didn't place any value on their children's education. When I saw such don't-care attitudes, I was thankful that my mother had been "education crazy."

In addition to these problems, the constant put-downs of racism had taken their toll on the self-image of these students. It fostered a what's-the-use attitude toward learning or any other kind of self-improvement. At such a young age, the psychology of poverty was already tightening its grip around these impressionable minds.

So we decided to emphasize tutoring in English, math, black history, Bible, and art. We already had a good start in this direction, thanks to the work of Chris Erb, the white college student who had come to Mendenhall as a volunteer during the summer of 1969. Chris shared our concern about education for deprived children. She had continued to visit Simpson County each summer, developing the tutoring program and building a library for children.

Chris had remarkable courage, a lot of determination, and an unshakable faith. She needed every bit of it in those days because whenever she crossed the tracks into white Mendenhall, she met with hostility. Her first encounter with it was in the bank, where she and another volunteer had gone to cash a check. A bank officer recognized them as volunteers in the black community. "What are you doing here?" he demanded. "You're a bunch of communists! Who sent you—the Cubans?"

Then there were frequent stops by the police, who searched her car and questioned her about her presence in Mendenhall. The searches were always just a pretense. When she'd ask what the officers were looking for, they'd say, "Oh, there's been a lot of trouble around. We're just looking for whatever." Their attitude seemed to be, If we do this often enough, maybe she'll get the hint and leave.

I often wondered why she stayed, or for that matter why she had come to Mississippi in the first place. She told me that it began when she was in high school at a small Quaker boarding school in Pennsylvania. She'd grown up in a comfortable, middle-class home in a predominantly white northern city. She'd been taught that all men and women are equal in God's sight, but that idea was untested since she'd rarely met anyone different from her. Her school had only three black students out of several hundred whites.

One day at school she saw a *Life* magazine picture of a group of rowdy-looking white men, mouths stuffed with chewing tobacco, guffawing and grinning at each other as though they were watching a funny movie. But the photo wasn't taken in a movie theater—it was in a courtroom. The men were on trial for the murder of three civil rights workers the previous summer. When she saw their expressions, Chris said she was shocked because they were acting like their crime was a big joke.

A concern for the rights of black people began to grow inside her. She felt concern over their poverty and the injustice shown them. Then, in 1969, the American Friends Service Committee, a Quaker organization, offered her a chance to use her teaching skills as a volunteer in Mississippi. That's when I met her.

Now she was a vital part of our efforts to break the cycle of poverty by preparing young people to attend integrated schools.

We faced an uphill battle. "Last night I attended a PTA meeting," Chris told me one morning. "It was supposedly held to discuss integration plans. But the white man running the meeting was very patronizing. He spoke down to the blacks in the audience, first-naming everyone and publicly reminding them of the various debts they owed him, financial and otherwise. He also kept dodging questions by saying that nobody is exactly sure 'just what the courts want.'" Chris was shocked by the whole affair, but I'd seen it all before.

"Chris, they're going to do everything they can to maintain a policy of noncompliance," I told her. "That's why your program is all the more vital. We've got to do all we can to fill in the gaps for black children in our area."

"The gaps are pretty big!" she replied. "I've learned that Mississippi has been spending five times more to educate white children than black children!"

Gaps like that made our feeble efforts look pretty insignificant. Our outreach was to the poorest children in the county, who lived far away on the most rutted dirt roads, and all we had to reach them were beat-up vans that ran on bald tires, with recycled engines that broke down repeatedly. Sometimes we didn't have enough typewriters for the typing students. Often we didn't even have enough chairs or books or even pencils.

But we didn't let this stop us. Workers like Chris showed incredible dedication. Sometimes she worked around the clock when children visited her in a little barbershop that she had turned into volunteer quarters.

"The four Magee youngsters came to my door last night about eight-thirty," she told me one day. "Donnie is in our second grade class, and Kit and Yvette come to the library. Nate sometimes comes with them, but he's only four. They told me they had had nothing to eat, so I made a macaroni-and-tomato casserole for them. They ate it all—even licked their paper plates and the frying pan! After I fed them, I sent them home. But at ten-thirty they were back, much to my surprise. 'Where's your father?' I asked them.

"'He's drunk,' Donnie told me.

"I put them all to bed. Dolphus, I found out that the only meals they're getting are the ones at public school and the one at tutoring class. Nate doesn't even get those! He's so skinny. But I think all of them are suffering from malnutrition.'"

I thought of how many kids I'd seen like that in Simpson County.

Chris continued. "I guess they live with their father. I don't know why he doesn't take care of them!" she said with obvious disgust.

I told her I would see what I could find out about the situation. A few days later she stopped by. "I've got some background on the Magees," I told her. "The mother brought the four younger children to live with their father and three teenage brothers and then left. The father works two jobs—one at the pulp mill and another on irregular shifts at a factory about fifteen miles from here. From what I've heard, the whole system has just about destroyed him. All his life he's been told that he's a nobody, and I guess he believes it."

Chris said, "I guess I have no business judging him. I can't imagine what it must be like to come from that background. But it seems like even less fortunate people than he have been able to rise above their circumstances. You did! And you're so important as a role model to the children around here. You show them that they can be somebody."

I felt a surge of affirmation when I heard that. One of the reasons I had come back to Mendenhall was so that I could contribute something positive to the situation. When a community has few good role models, the ones who suffer are the kids because they start wanting to be like whatever role models they see. I felt proud to think that God was using me to show kids in Simpson County that it was possible to rise above their circumstances.

"I wish there were a lot more role models," I sighed. "I wish some of those guys who went up North and out West looking for better jobs would come back. Young boys, especially, need them to look up to."

In the meantime, I told her, the tutoring program was vitally important to the children's future and their self-esteem. I was also glad that she introduced them to books about black leaders and black history, books that gave them pride in their heritage and influenced their families as well. Above all, I was impressed that she showed the children Christian love and kindness outside of class, the way she had with the four Magee children that night.

Chris told me how one Sunday they had come to her house as she was getting ready to go to church. "Would you like to go with me?" she asked them.

"Yeah!" they cried. Then Donnie, the oldest, asked, "Can we go like this?" "This" was dirty, ill-fitting clothes with holes. Chris took them anyhow.

Feeling compassion for Nate, she began to cook lunch for him. "His condition really came through to me when I asked him, 'What do you want to do today?'" she told me. "I thought he'd say 'Color,' or 'Look at picture books,' or 'Play with the puppies.' Instead he just said, 'Eat!'"

Nate wasn't alone in his need for decent food. Many of the kids we were working with in the tutoring program had difficulty with even the most simple tasks. Their attention span was short, and they fell asleep at their desks. We discovered that often they had only potato chips or a cookie to eat, instead of a hot, nutritious meal. Sometimes, like Nate, they had nothing. We began to provide them with one well-balanced meal each day, using vegetables and fruits we grew ourselves on land that old Mr. Buckley (recall him from chapter 5) let us use for this purpose.

Chris proved invaluable in working with kids like the Magee children. But she was only able to be with us during the summers. During the rest of the year we tried to target young people who had not had the benefit of Chris's tutoring.

One such girl—I'll call her Franci—had almost flunked out of school, not because she lacked intelligence, but because she had a low estimate of what she could do. At home she'd been told, "You can't do it, so don't worry about it," instead of, "You can do it! You've got to do it!"

Rosie and I sat down with her and helped her set two goals: to attend school without missing a single day, and to make the honor roll. For a while she had no problem achieving the first goal. As long as we were around, reminding her of her commitment, she didn't miss a single day of school. Eventually our pressure became her own. She began to choose not to miss. But one day she was sick and had to stay home. That seemed to get her off the track because soon a little bad attitude began to creep in, and she began to find other excuses to miss. I began to travel more and wasn't always around to check her progress. Before long she'd missed five days.

As for her honor roll attempt, she worked hard during the first semester and came close. But a low grade in one subject cost her the goal. Later, as I thought about why, I realized that she'd heard too much praise like "Look how much better you are from last year!" That's bad reinforcement when last year was only *D*'s and *F*'s. It was not enough to compare her performance to the previous year. Instead, the real question she needed to answer was, Have I done my best?

A more successful student was Marlene. As she participated in the tutoring program, we watched her develop from a shy, withdrawn person into a leader who was able to help with tutoring younger children. Later, we were thrilled to see her graduate from college and begin working as a vital part of the community. Her success became a powerful role model to the other young who desperately needed it. Best of all, she never forgot the ministry and the deep impact it had had on her life. She caught a vision for how she could use her education to reach out and help others. She showed us all that the dream could become reality!

Marlene stands in contrast to a young man who was going to drop out of high school and start hauling pulpwood. He became a Christian through the witness of Herbert, myself, and others. Then, after getting help in our tutoring program, he went on to college and played football there. When he needed money, we found him a job to earn it. But when he returned to school, we didn't hear from him again until he came home during the next school break. Eventually he graduated and went elsewhere to work. We were glad that we'd helped him escape the poverty he'd grown up in. But we were also disappointed that he never caught a vision for helping other potential dropouts.

Not all the problems were academic. One girl was very bright. She made all *A*'s and was very attractive. She worked for us part-time while she went to high school. But one day she came in for counseling. She was devastated—and pregnant.

"I'm going to commit suicide!" she threatened. "I don't feel like living. What will people think of me? What will I think of myself? I was the queen! A top student! And look at me now!" Despair spilled out of her.

"You and God are going to make it," I assured her.

"As long as my boyfriend doesn't leave me, I'll make it!" she responded.

"No, you and God are going to make it," I repeated.

A few weeks later her boyfriend dropped her, and she hit bottom.

"Nobody loves me!" she cried. Her parents were teachers, and she felt from their disappointment that they didn't love her. "They like me to make *A*'s! They like to see me on the honor roll! But they don't love me now! I'm hurting them!"

I repeated my earlier promise: "You and God are going to make it!"

"Maybe as long as I work at the ministry I'll make it," she countered.

"No! It's you and God!"

A few weeks later the elders of the church, who oversaw the ministry, decided that she should stop working until after the baby was born. That devastated her.

As we talked together, I tried to lend some new perspective. "God and you are much stronger than all those other girls who had babies but don't have God in their lives. They made it. Surely with God's help you can make it."

Finally she got the message. She couldn't attend school, but she studied at home, took her tests, and graduated with her class. Then she went on to college—and graduated with flying colors! She also took responsibility for raising her child. Today she's a productive person in the community.

One of my goals in our work with the young people was that every one of them would gain something through their contact with our ministry. Obviously I hoped that all of them would become children of God with a passion to grow spiritually. But that didn't always happen. Still, most were at least helped to develop skills that would help them make it in life financially and not end up as failures. Many others participated simply because they got something they didn't get at home.

In addition to the tutoring, we developed a summer program to encourage students with college potential as well as those already in college. A typical day started with everyone getting up at five to go work at the farm until eight or eight-thirty. After breakfast and washing up, there was free time before lunch. Then came two hours of tutoring in math, reading, black history, and typing. We mixed in some local field trips and even made overnight trips to Memphis and New Orleans. For many of the kids involved, these trips were their first opportunity to travel away from Simpson County. Seeing new places and sights expanded their outlook.

We planned the program so that we could pay these students a small stipend toward their college expenses. At first it was thirty-five dollars a week, but later we increased it to sixty-five a week—a lot of money for us! At the end of the summer we asked them, "How much money have you saved?" In every case we got the same answer: "Nothing!"

Amazed, we asked what they'd done with their money and found that most had wasted it. But in a few cases parents had said, "Loan us some of it. We'll pay you back at schooltime." But instead of paying it back, the parents replied, "We've been paying for you for a long time. Now it's our turn to enjoy!" The loans never got repaid.

That taught us that we needed a different method of payment. More important, we needed to teach the students how to handle money in a responsible way. So the second year we gave them half of their stipend outright and put the other half in a college scholarship fund. Students already in college or going to college at the end of the summer received the full amount toward school expenses when they left for school. For high school students we kept the money in the fund until they were ready for college. If they ended up not going to college, we gave them the money when they graduated from high school.

To pay for this program we used the students' work at the farm. We found that if they worked twenty acres planted with peas, watermelon, okra, and corn as cash crops, we could usually raise enough to pay them.

We also began to bring in college students from other parts of the country and match them one-on-one with the local kids. Our hope was that through this interaction, our kids would discover ways to improve themselves and their community. When word got around about this opportunity, kids from all over Simpson County wanted to participate.

Despite all of these efforts, however, we noticed that many kids in black Mendenhall were constantly getting into trouble. They'd wander the streets, breaking windows, vandalizing cars, getting into fights. As we looked into the situation, we found that many of them had no place to vent their energies or spend their time.

We asked ourselves, What do more affluent communities provide to keep their kids out of trouble? Typically they have a YMCA or YWCA, a boys' and girls' club, sports teams, and so forth from which the kids could choose. In addition, their families often provided them with music lessons and similar opportunities. Plus they had transportation to and from these activities.

When we looked at our own community, we realized that we had none of this. So we came up with the idea to start a recreation center, or better yet, a multipurpose building. As we worked on a design for it, we decided that in addition to a gymnasium, we wanted classrooms on the side for tutoring and the like. We also realized that such a facility would be a fantastic gathering place for a youth ministry. We figured that if we planned our programs carefully, there was no reason why we couldn't have fifty or seventy-five kids coming together every Saturday night to sing songs and to be challenged with the gospel.

So we set about drawing up plans for the structure, raising the money, and hiring a contractor. In 1972 we dedicated the R. A. Buckley Center. Right away it became a cornerstone for our programs. It did far more than give our young people a place to play and learn. It offered them a symbol of hope, a visible reminder that someone cared about them and was there to help. The facility broke new ground in Mendenhall. It showed the entire community—both blacks and whites—that change was at hand. Something good could happen for blacks. They didn't have to settle for second best. But the new facility was only the beginning!

100

E L E V E N

ALL ABOUT HEALTH—

AND MIRACLES

When I was a boy, our family never thought of taking a sick person to see a doctor. There were no black doctors, and we didn't feel welcome in the white clinics. Besides, even if we'd wanted to get professional care, we could never have afforded it. (And of course we didn't have health insurance.) So Mama would treat our aches and pains with home remedies that she'd learned from her mother and grandmother. Nobody expected anything different.

When I returned to Mississippi in 1971, things hadn't changed much. Black folks were still without adequate health care. Dave Lousma, a dental student volunteering in the ministry that summer, surveyed the county and found a lot of black folks who had never been to a dentist. Many declared they'd never see a doctor unless they were so sick someone had to carry them in. Those who had gone recalled the discouragement and humiliation they'd felt sitting in segregated waiting rooms, watching all the white people receive care first.

As I thought about this situation, I felt that accessible, affordable health care was a basic necessity that blacks in Mendenhall shouldn't have to do without. So we began to consider what it would take to meet this need. During the next year or so, the vision of a cooperative health center took shape.

We had no idea how to get such a facility built, let alone staffed. But we began to pray, learn, and plan.

Soon God brought to our staff Erv and Joan Huston. Erv was a minister, and Joan was a registered nurse. We realized that her expertise would be invaluable in helping us bring our dream into reality. In fact, we took her presence as a signal that God wanted us to move ahead on a cooperative health center.

So we started construction on a building to house it. Even though we didn't have a doctor, we wanted to be ready when God brought that person to us! In addition, we asked Dr. Kevin Lake from California to come for two weeks to screen potential patients and set up information files on them. We had faith!

And during the winter of 1973-74 God sent us Dr. Charles Fraley, a missionary planning to go to Tanzania. He agreed to join us on an interim basis while waiting for his visa. So we had our doctor—for a while, anyway.

Meanwhile, we campaigned to raise $13,000 to buy X-ray equipment. Within three months we had the funds, and the equipment was installed. On the afternoon of April 11, 1974, Dr. Fraley tested it—on me!

I left the clinic brimming with excitement over God's provision for the equipment, the facility, and the doctor. I looked forward to leading the dedication ceremonies for this long-awaited event the next day. Unfortunately, it looked like Mississippi's spring was going to rain on our party; drops were already falling as I headed home.

All night the rains came down. In fact, it rained harder and longer that night than either Rosie or I could recall. By morning I started to worry. Mendenhall's "black quarters," as white people had always called our section of town, lies in a crook of Sellers Creek that drains into the Pearl River. From time out of mind that creek has flooded when the spring rains are heavy. It still does to this day. Minor flooding happens nearly every year. Major floods, with water standing five inches to five feet in every house and building in town, happen once or twice every decade.

The problem is that the channel in the creek is not deep enough to handle heavy runoff, so it backs up and floods us out. The U.S. Army Corps of Engineers and others have studied the situation. But no action has ever been taken. As a result, we lived then and we live now with an annual threat of flooding.

Occasionally someone asks me why we don't just move. It's the same question as to why folks don't just move out of a ghetto in a big city. Where would we move? And how could our people afford it? Most important, why should they have to? Their houses may not be worth much, and some of them are barely adequate to shelter the families that live in them, but they still represent home. I suppose someone could come along and donate land and houses for relocation, and that might be fantastic. But if you compare the cost of that to the cost of deepening the creek, it makes more sense to deepen the creek.

At any rate, I awoke with a bad feeling about the amount of water flowing in the nearby creek. I knew we were going to have at least minor flooding. What really scared me was what might happen to the clinic and the equipment.

I called John Perkins in Jackson and alerted him to the situation. Then the other staff members and I frantically began to move what was movable to the higher shelves and cabinets. But it seemed like there just weren't enough high places. And we couldn't do anything about our new X-ray machine. So instead of dedicating it that day, we stood and watched helplessly as the muddy, swirling water inevitably rose and submerged its vital parts.

But the flood didn't stop there. It also invaded the multipurpose center, the tutoring rooms, and a new co-op store with all its merchandise.

As I trudged through the waters from building to building to check on the situation, my thoughts suddenly turned toward my own home. Rosie was alone there, nine months pregnant and due any day. I needed to check on her. So I made my way to our house. I felt sick when I saw the water surging toward our door. Inside, a frightened Rosie had wakened with a shock to see water covering the yard.

"What are we going to do?" she cried as I rushed into the house.

"There's nothing we can do but get out fast!" I yelled. Fortunately, she had already packed a bag for her trip to the hospital. With one hand I grabbed it, and with the other I steadied her as we waded through the water that was already spilling under the door.

"Our house!" she cried. "The floors will be ruined!" It was a pitiful moment. Only months before we'd moved into this house. Before, we'd lived in a run-down, two-room house that had holes in every wall and no doors on the closets. This house felt like a dream house by comparison. Seeing it swallowed up in water was too much to take, and as I pulled her away she broke into tears.

Rosie wasn't the only one crying. We joined dozens of other homeless families heading for higher ground, watching the little that they possessed wash away. Later the town had to open its armory as an emergency shelter for all of us.

The next morning John Perkins and I stood on the railroad tracks and looked down on the depressing sight. I looked toward the submerged clinic and thought about all the five-, ten-, and twenty-dollar gifts that had made it possible. What a waste! We had worked and prayed so hard to provide a simple clinic so that black folks in Simpson County wouldn't have to rely on folk medicine to get by. And overnight it was gone! I suddenly felt the trapped feeling again, the one I'd come to know at an early age. I felt empty. I had no fight left to draw on.

But then John reminded me of the homeless in the armory. Most had been poor to begin with. Now they had nothing. Where would they go? What would they eat? What would they wear? We realized we had to take action to deal with the immediate crisis; we could worry about the future—and the clinic—later.

So we organized our staff people and other helpers. The first thing we did was pray. Then I was named chairman of the Community Disaster Committee. In the next few days, as the water slowly receded, we surveyed the flood victims, recording the extent of their losses for the Red Cross and for the mayor of Mendenhall, who applied to the governor for disaster aid.

A week after the flood, Rosie gave birth to our first child, a beautiful little girl whom we named Danita. I felt so proud, but I also was worried for Rosie. The house she'd left a few days before was not the same one she was bringing her new baby home to! Her new washing machine, installed only three days before the flood, had been badly damaged. The water had risen to four feet inside, leaving mud on her beautiful hardwood floors and dirty water lines on her freshly painted walls. I scrubbed for hours but couldn't get the stains off. Worst of all, the house smelled dank and musty. Rosie didn't want to bring a newborn into a house that wasn't as sanitary as it should be.

So she appealed to the community health department to come and sanitize it, but they never did. But despite her worried parents and her less-than-perfect homecoming, Danita managed just fine.

About a month after the flood, Dr. Fraley received his visa to go to Tanzania. We'd known all along that he was only temporary, but the timing of his departure hit us hard. We teased him by saying, "Why do you want to go to Africa? Look around! You're already in Africa!" But in the end we said our good-byes. I hurt to see him go. Where would we find a replacement? God gave us some relief by providing Dr. Henry Lowen from Kansas. Hearing of our plight, he came for a month while we stepped up our search for a permanent doctor. But with little result.

We made inquiries all over, but we couldn't seem to find just the right person. We did find people who were technically competent. But they didn't share our Christian convictions. When we shared this with our mailing list, we received back letters saying, "As scarce as doctors are, you'd better quit praying for a Christian doctor and just pray for a doctor!" That forced us to ask: Should we take just any doctor, or were we going to trust God to send us a Christian doctor? Did it matter? We weren't sure what to do.

Those were hard days in the ministry. The flooding of the clinic, coupled with the loss of Dr. Fraley, put everyone in a gloomy mood. We'd all felt so enthusiastic about having a facility right in our own community, with our own doctor and everything. Now the dream seemed as far away as ever. It sounded like a repeat of the same old story: Black people couldn't do anything successful, and if they did, it couldn't last.

Then we suffered insult on top of our injury: our hazard insurance on the ministry's property didn't cover flood damage! Our only consolation was that a new policy at least covered the clinic.

There was only one thing to do—pray! So we organized prayer meetings and cried out to God for some light in the midst of the gloom that hung over our staff and the rest of the black community.

We also redoubled our efforts to get a clinic going again. One of the first things to decide, of course, was where we were going to locate it. We didn't want it to ever get flooded out again. So

105

one opinion was that we should move it out of the "black quarters" into white Mendenhall.

I didn't like that at all. "Our goal has always been to have medical services located in the black community," I argued. "Besides, how are we going to get a building? We tried to get a building downtown for a thrift store, and nobody would sell to us."

"That may be," I heard, "but it's just too low here. You can't afford to have this happen again. That X-ray equipment cost a lot to buy the first time, and a lot to repair after the flood. Who's going to pay for fixing it the next time?"

I knew it was true. The solution that made the most sense was to get the creek channel deepened. But I knew that was even more remote than getting a building across the tracks. So, like it or not, the fear of another flood pushed us toward relocating the clinic to the higher ground of white Mendenhall.

As we surveyed available properties, an empty medical building across from the courthouse caught our eye. It had been vacant for years because the doctor who built it didn't want to see it used for anything but a medical clinic. He'd practiced in it until his death. Since then his widow had been unable to find a suitable buyer.

We approached her about purchasing it, and our timing couldn't have been better. She desperately wanted to see her husband's dream continued. So finally she sold it to us, despite pressures from some in the white community not to do so.

The purchase gave us a bit of hope after the flood. But we weren't home yet. We still had to find a doctor. If getting a building had taken one miracle, getting a doctor to practice in it was going to require another.

But God showered many miracles during that period. A group of young people from the First Presbyterian Church of Colorado Springs visited us. Hearing about our doctorless clinic, they joined us in a day of fasting and prayer about the situation. Then they returned to Colorado Springs, where they came across a doctor who had just come out of the military and had no particular plans for where he wanted to practice.

"God wants you in Mississippi!" they cried. So convincing were they that the doctor, wanting to be open to God's leading, decided he'd better check us out. Dr. Eugene McCarty and his wife, Joann, came to look us over. After discussion and prayer, they committed themselves to Mendenhall for two years. Another miracle! The clinic was to be a reality after all!

This time our dedication ceremonies came off without a hitch. And, because the facility was opening in white Mendenhall, it was appropriate to have the mayor attend. Other representatives from the white business and professional community were invited, but none came. Still, we were achieving our goal of establishing a clinic that would serve the black community of Simpson County. Now the question remained: Would they come? Furthermore, would white patients come? As it turned out, both came. We learned that the location of the clinic didn't matter nearly as much as its reputation for serving the needs of the poor, whether black or white.

Rosie and I have been among those who have benefited most from having access to that kind of care. In late 1975 Rosie was pregnant again. But early tests revealed that the fetus, likely a male, had a genetic problem known as G6PD, a serious anemia carried by mothers and transmitted mainly to male offspring. A genetic counselor in Jackson told her that the best thing she could do would be to have an abortion.

That didn't sound right to us, so we returned to Mendenhall and went to see Dr. McCarty. He proved to be God's man for our situation. We discovered that he had concentrated on genetics in his training. After researching the literature, he was able to tell us that black males were less susceptible to this particular genetic problem than white males. Therefore, our baby's chances of being normal were higher.

We took this information as a signal from God that we should continue the pregnancy. On July 16 Rosie gave birth to a boy—a completely healthy, normal boy. We named him Reggie. And we were ecstatic. He was our first son, and the first male among all the Weary family, so he could carry on the name. Moreover, the availability and expertise of Dr. McCarty had had a direct bearing on his delivery. Even ten years earlier, blacks like ourselves could never have gotten that kind of professional opinion in Simpson County.

We never forgot, though, that Dr. McCarty would only be with us for two years. We were eager to find a permanent doctor. So we continued to pray that God would provide one—and to spread the word everywhere that we needed one. One day I spoke at a church in Newark, New Jersey, and mentioned our need. After the service, a young black man introduced himself as Dennis Adams.

"I was sitting in the audience while you spoke, wondering where I could live out my faith and use my medical training. What's this about needing a doctor?"

"Are you a doctor?" I asked excitedly.

"Well, not quite. I'm nearly finished with med school, but I still have my residency to go."

Was this our man? I began praying for guidance for both of us. I also told him more about our clinic and our overall vision of establishing an oasis of hope there in Simpson County. I knew he was genuinely interested because he asked a lot of intelligent questions. I stressed the need for a commitment to the clinic over a period of time, as well as the value of having a black physician as a role model to the young people in the community. After a good exchange, we agreed to keep in touch. He promised to consider prayerfully whether God wanted him to commit himself to the Mendenhall community.

Later he visited us in Mississippi, and eventually he told us he and his wife, Judi, had decided to move to Mendenhall as soon as he completed his residency. And so, after Dr. McCarty's faithful service to us for two years, Dr. Adams became our first permanent doctor. We knew that would mean a lot to the patients to have someone they could relate to over many years. Furthermore, as the first black doctor in Mendenhall, he became a significant symbol to everyone in town.

We took advantage of this and recruited five young black people to work in the clinic. After school let out at three, they would arrive for their duties at three-thirty. We trained two of them to be nurses aides, two to be lab technicians, and one to keep the books and handle clerical duties. It was an outstanding opportunity for leadership development. Today, one is a secretary for the school system, one is a registered nurse, one is a medical technologist, one is a physician, and Billy, who kept the books, went to college and majored in business and accounting. The clinic enabled them to develop a vision for their lives as well as practical skills to use in the marketplace.

I was so grateful to God for providing the resources of Dr. Adams and the clinic. Access to that kind of care had been unimaginable to me growing up. After the flood and all we'd been through, having it seemed like an impossible dream come true. But once it was in place, God decided to test whether my confidence in medical technology had become greater than my confidence in Him.

In 1983 we took a family vacation to Colorado. On our way home we stopped in Dallas, where I had to attend a board meeting for a sister ministry starting there called Voice of Hope. While we were there we noticed that Reggie's breathing began to change and he began wheezing. A doctor couldn't pinpoint the problem but recommended that we have him checked more intensively as soon as we returned to Mendenhall.

Dr. Adams didn't like what he saw. Reggie's neck was swelling, so he administered antibiotics. But when the condition didn't change, he recommended a hospital in Jackson that could carry out a more extensive diagnosis. Yet even after various tests were run and more antibiotics were given, Reggie's neck continued to swell. His nasal passages couldn't drain, and he had great difficulty breathing. Baffled pediatricians, hematologists, and oncologists studied the test findings, including a biopsy. Rosie and I were filled with anxiety. Finally we were given a diagnosis: non-Hodgkins lymphoma, a malignancy of the lymph nodes.

It took a while for what I heard to soak in. *Cancer? It can't be!* I thought. *It's just a resistant virus, that's all.* But I was just in denial. Reggie was very sick, sick enough to die. And the doctors could only tell us they'd do the best they could, but they couldn't make any guarantees. When the impact of it all finally hit me, I felt nauseous and wanted to cry. But I kept thinking, *I can't cry; I've got to be strong for Rosie!*

But it was Rosie who seemed strong and in charge of her feelings, though it was really numbness, she told me later. During a painful bone marrow test on Reggie, she stayed in the room, which didn't surprise me because I knew she was the strongest when it came to dealing with the kids' illnesses. But after a while she left.

I found her in the hall sobbing. "I can't stay in there and watch him go through it!"

I tried to comfort her, but how could I? I was no more able to deal with Reggie's pain than she was. I could barely handle my own pain. Even as I held her, I was crying out to God, *Why? Why?* And in the same moment I felt ashamed. *Where's my faith?* I wondered. *I'm a Christian, a seminary graduate—and I'm questioning God!*

In the days that followed, we both struggled with our emotions and confusion. Somehow during that awful time, God broke through my questions and hurt and reminded me, "Dolphus, I still love you. I still care for you." As for Rosie, she felt angry at Him for allowing this to happen. But then one day she was walking around the hospital and noticed other sick children. Some of them had cancer, too, just like Reggie. And she realized that they also had parents who loved them and wanted to hold onto them.

"It hit me that we're no more special than the parents of those children," she told me. "Why should we think trials are just for others, that we should be spared?"

Still, she admitted that she could hardly pray. Fortunately, others were on their knees on her behalf. Rosie was scared. "I'm afraid our baby's going to die, Dolphus!" She swallowed hard, fighting the tears. "I don't know if I can take that."

"Rosie, we've got to give it to God!" I felt as weak and doubtful as she did, but we prayed together, and Rosie's prayer was, "Lord, not my will but thine be done." We asked God to strengthen Reggie as he endured the painful tests and treatments, and for Danita and ourselves to hold up. We also prayed for the doctors, for wisdom and skill. We realized that they were merely tools in God's hands to provide for Reggie's physical needs. We were grateful for them, but in the end it was God who would determine the outcome.

In the following days God showed us in so many ways that He was with us, that He cared for us, no matter what happened. He gave a lot of fight and courage to our weak, frightened little boy—as well as to that little boy's weak and frightened parents.

A verse in James seemed especially comforting: "Consider it pure joy, my brothers, whenever you face trials of many kinds, because you know that the testing of your faith develops perseverance" (1:2-4, NIV). We definitely needed to develop some perseverance!

During this ordeal, countless friends rallied around us, not only black friends, but white friends in Jackson, too. One white couple, Louis and Helen Ridgway, learned that we had no place to stay during Reggie's ten-week hospitalization. They told us, "Our home is your home. What else can we do to help?" They visited the hospital, provided meals, and demonstrated a compassion that seemed to say, "We love you. We care about you. We want to be available for you."

During this period I began traveling more and more to explain our work in Mendenhall to churches and other interested groups. I always invited questions following my presentation. At a white church in another part of the country, a man got up and said, "I think you should just preach the gospel and not get involved in economic and social matters." In response I tried to explain to him that because of years of poverty and segregation, few blacks had any economic base in their communities. "I don't believe that Christ called us to ignore ills that keep blacks down," I said. I don't know whether I convinced him or not. But afterward I realized how upset I'd felt by his question.

As I reflected on the incident, I realized how strongly I felt about Reggie's illness and its treatment. The normal way that poor people in poor communities treat sickness is to call grandmother. Grandmother's supposed to know how to treat fevers. She'll tell them to take the baby and bathe him in cool water and apply various ointments and folk remedies and such, and after two or three days, the fever is supposed go away.

We weren't doing things the old way in Mendenhall anymore. And the reason was precisely because we had a heart to meet social needs as well as spiritual ones. And God had blessed that by providing a doctor, so that instead of calling grandmother, we could call a doctor and get Reggie to some help. Without it, he would probably have died—like so many black children did when I was growing up.

So the man's question had burst a bubble of emotion, an awesome feeling that sometimes we do things a certain way only because we have no other options. Because of God's concern for social justice and social services, we now had options in our town. I didn't want anybody to threaten them or question their legitimacy!

In early October Reggie came home—minus all of his hair as a result of the treatment. Three weeks later he was allowed to go back to school, as long as he took extra care to avoid colds because his resistance was so low. He continued on medication until March, when all signs of the illness disappeared. By the grace of God, Reggie was well!

T W E L V E

LEARNING ABOUT

MIRACLES OF LEARNING

Every day as I went about my work, I passed an abandoned, two-story, cinder-block building. The windows were broken out. The weeds were so high they looked like they wanted to devour it. It was a real eyesore. But far worse than its appearance was what it stood for, at least to me. Every time I saw it I remembered that it had been an all-black school during the days of segregation. In fact, I had attended fifth and sixth grades there. But now it reminded me of how much blacks in Mississippi lost when the schools were integrated.

Don't misunderstand! Integration gave countless black children access to many of the same resources available to whites. No one should discount that. But the way integration was carried out cost blacks a lot, too. For instance, my old high school, Harper High, was one of three black high schools during the segregation era. But when the county finally desegregated its school system, all three were made into middle schools and their names were changed. Harper had been named for its founder, a black professor. It became Mendenhall Junior High. New Hymn, named after a black church, New Hymn Baptist, was renamed Simpson Central School. Likewise, McLaurin was renamed Magee Junior High. Here were these institutions that had roots and a cultural history, and all of that was lost through integration.

We also lost two of our three black principals. The federal government said that one of the three high schools had to have a black principal. But that put the other two out of work. What a tragic loss of desperately needed black male leadership and black male role models! Furthermore, our children had to leave their own turf and cross the tracks and go up to white Mendenhall for classes. That reinforced the idea that education was something that only happened among whites; if a black person wanted it, he'd have to go to the whites to get it. Beyond all that, integration placed our children in a system that was becoming increasingly secular.

Somehow the abandoned schoolhouse always reminded me of these things. It had been the original Harper High. Black folks had patched together five- and ten-dollar contributions to buy the property where it sat and the individual blocks from which it was built. It had been the first school for blacks in Simpson County. Now it was abandoned.

So I took my thoughts and feelings and turned them into a prayer: *Lord, what should I be doing about the education of black children in Simpson County? You know that most of them are behind from the start of their schooling. How will they ever catch up? And those who stay in school are learning a lot of values that seem opposed to your ways. What can I do about this?* For years I prayed prayers like that, and I wondered whether God would ever answer them.

If someone had given me a blank check, I would have refurbished that empty building and turned it into a Christian school. But no blank checks ever arrived, and I knew whatever we did would have to start on a small scale. The idea of a preschool seemed appealing.

A local Head Start program sponsored a nursery school for children of very low-income parents. But people who earned between $7,000 and $12,000 a year were not eligible to send their youngsters there. No black church operated such a program, and the white churches wouldn't allow black children to attend theirs. So in 1976 we began talking about a nursery school for children of low-income parents.

While we were in the middle of our planning, two graduates of Wheaton College in Wheaton, Illinois, contacted us. One had a degree in early childhood education and the other in elementary education. Would we be interested in starting a school in Mendenhall? they asked us. Out of the blue, it seemed like maybe God was answering my prayers!

So Steve Hayes and Debbie Hale moved to town and began doing the research necessary to establish a viable school. For six months they analyzed the local school system and the geographical location of the parents of young children, among other data. When they finished, they opened a nursery school for two- and three-year-olds whose parents attended Mendenhall Bible Church, the church over our ministry.

Then in the fall they introduced the first real kindergarten, with thirteen children enrolled for half-day sessions. The name they gave to this program was Genesis One Kindergarten—connoting a biblical idea of education "from the beginning." We limited the program to four- and five-year-olds and, because so many parents worked, we offered it all day.

We faced two hurdles in winning acceptance for Genesis One Kindergarten. First, many parents had trouble with the idea of children going to school before they were six. They'd always been told that children start school at six, and that was that. A second problem was that parents weren't used to paying for education. We knew they couldn't afford to pay much, so we only charged six dollars a week per child and made up the difference through fund-raising efforts.

I was thrilled to see children beginning to learn and feel good about themselves. The very existence of the school communicated that it was OK to learn, that someone cared about them, and that education was a possibility for them. Maybe I'd inherited my mother's bent of being "education crazy." But I was overjoyed that these kids were getting a good start.

Of course, the real test of the program's effectiveness would be how well our "graduates" did when they moved into first grade at the public school. Thanks to Steve and Debbie's excellent work, the transition went smoothly for all of them. When the schools tested incoming first graders, our children earned high ratings.

So we weren't surprised when some of the parents in town started asking us, "Why don't you have a first grade, too? If you do, we'll support it!"

That sounded encouraging. But who would lead the effort to start such a program? Who knew enough about it? Where would the teachers come from? And where would we house such a school? I never forgot the abandoned schoolhouse, but it was in terrible shape. Where would we ever get the money to fix it up? All in all, the dream of a Christian grade school looked like it would have to remain just that for a while—an impossible dream!

But for years I kept praying that God would do something to make that dream a reality. I'd seen Him accomplish so much through the youth program, the clinic, the nursery school, and other arms of the ministry. Why not a school, too? But I knew that if anything was going to happen, it would have to be His doing.

Then one day, Judi Adams, the wife of Dr. Dennis Adams, asked me, "Dolphus, what's the outlook for a Genesis One primary school?"

I knew that Judi had been interested in this idea for a long time. She'd played a part in the kindergarten program. But before I could answer she told me, "Our children benefited so much from Genesis One Kindergarten. But they're not doing as well in public school."

We discussed the problem for a few minutes, and finally I explained my predicament. "I'd love to expand beyond a kindergarten, Judi. But there are so many things standing in the way. I mean, first we've got to be sure there's even a need. And that's going to take someone with time and know-how to do the research."

"Maybe I can help." she replied. "One of my majors in college was in childhood education. And I've had experience in the New York City school system."

This was unexpected good news. That—and her willingness—signaled to me that perhaps at last the Lord wanted us to take some exploratory steps toward a grade school.

So Judi went to work. She began with a telephone survey to find out what the area offered besides public school at the elementary level. Repeatedly she found policies that prevented black children from participating in private white schools, both secular and Christian. This, despite nine years of integration in the public schools!

She also found out that in a state ranked dead last in education, black children were at the absolute bottom in their level of skills at the first grade level. Many were seven or older in first grade, and few came from kindergartens because they were not offered by the public school system. Moreover, black children were dropping out of school at earlier ages than white children. School was compulsory only through the fifth grade, and even then the law was not enforced at the lower levels, especially when it came to blacks. Unless this changed, uneducated blacks would be forever destined to remain at the bottom academically and economically. I longed to see us do something to bring about such change in Simpson County.

Armed with this kind of information, Judi approached black parents. Would they be interested in sending their children to a Christian school that offered grades one through three and—Lord willing—someday the upper grades as well? The parents whose children had attended Genesis One Kindergarten were definitely interested. So were those who'd heard about Genesis One and who weren't satisfied with their children's progress in the public school.

But they had one major concern—the cost of tuition. That was our concern, too. We estimated that primary education would cost about $1,400 a year per child. In an area where the median income was barely above $6,000, there was no way people could afford it. Could they afford $525 a year if we could raise the $900 difference? Enough parents believed in the school to give it a try. The question remained: Were there enough concerned people willing to contribute to a sponsorship program? We began telling everyone we knew what we hoped to do and moved ahead.

As we thought about what we wanted to accomplish with this program, something I'd read somewhere kept coming to my mind: "No money or time is wasted that is invested in the life of a child." That was a powerful challenge to me. And I felt it was consistent with the challenge for education that Moses gave to the people of Israel in Deuteronomy 6:4-9:

> O Israel, listen: Jehovah is our God, Jehovah alone. You must love Him with *all* your heart, soul, and might. And you must think constantly about these commandments I am giving you today. You must teach them to your children and talk about them when you are at home or out for a walk; at bedtime and the first thing in the morning.

> Tie them on your finger, wear them on your forehead,
> and write them on the doorposts of your house! (TLB)

We wanted to equip students academically and spiritually.
With this in mind we selected the A-Beka curriculum, designed
to give traditional academic instruction using the Bible as its
basis for truth. We hoped that with a good elementary school
foundation our children would not drop out in higher grades
but would continue their education and become community
and family leaders. We also wanted to give each child an opportunity to develop a relationship with God and apply His
principles to his or her daily life.

So in the fall of 1982 we formally expanded Genesis One
School to grades one through three. Twenty-five children attended the kindergarten program, and ten enrolled in the elementary classes.

The next summer, as we evaluated the program, we found
that there were many parents who wanted to enroll their children but couldn't afford the $525 tuition. We didn't want to
exclude anyone who couldn't pay. But neither could we offer
free programs. So we set up a work program in which one or
both parents could work in our ministry a certain number of
hours each week in exchange for their children's basic tuition.

In the fall we opened with a fourth grade added, and enrollment doubled to seventy students. This created a space problem, especially with plans for fifth and sixth grades underway.
We scattered classes in buildings throughout the community,
but that wouldn't work for long. Judi and the staff turned to
me. Where would we house this program? I found myself praying, *Lord, remember that abandoned schoolhouse? Is now the
time for You to return it to usefulness?* In my mind I could see a
renovated, functional building housing Genesis One School.
But the picture blurred a bit when I learned that restoring it
would take $25,000 at a minimum. Still, I hoped and prayed.

A few months later a group from Aurora Christian School in
Aurora, Illinois, came to help with various work projects. I
showed them the crowded Genesis One classes and shared my
dream for the run-down building. They took this as a bit of a
challenge and during their school's spring break sent 160 students and adults to work on the structure. Led by Paul House,

they transformed it from the eyesore that it was into something that looked a lot more like the one I envisioned. By week's end they had done all but a few small jobs. Their work was a fantastic gift!

Soon afterward a man named Reid Farmer brought a group from Second Presbyterian Church in Memphis, and they graded and fenced the playground. When Reid returned home, a woman in his church quizzed him about the school. Then she donated playground equipment costing $8,000. About the same time, a Jackson couple donated $10,000 for a kitchen. With that, our school was just about complete.

On August 10, 1984, we held dedication ceremonies in the multipurpose center down the street from the new building. It was the only facility large enough to handle the crowd of nearly five hundred. The mayor was there. Our board was there. The group from Aurora had come down. We sang hymns of praise, the choir performed some special numbers, and various folks gave testimonials.

Finally it was my turn to give the main address. I planned to center my remarks on the idea of the Genesis One building as an impossible dream that God had made into a reality. As I stood up and looked out on the audience I saw lots of friends there who had been a part of the vision from the beginning. I saw young people who had gone off to college and were starting to come back and offer their skills and resources to the community. I saw parents, some of whom had been skeptical about our efforts, but who were now solid supporters. I saw their children, who represented such a hope for the future. And suddenly, as I started working my way through my speech, I felt overwhelmed with emotion.

Genesis One School had been an impossible dream from the beginning. Yet it was now a reality. The building was there. The students were there. The funding was there. God had once again performed a miracle in Mendenhall, helping us to link up with people who wanted to buy in to the vision of creating hope where there had been no hope.

And that took me to an even greater intensity of feeling. Somehow the renovation of the Genesis One building convinced me that God really was behind our efforts. The fact is, I'd been something of a skeptic myself over the years. Even though I'd been away from Mendenhall and seen God do incredible things in my own life, and even though I'd seen him do incredible things in our ministry already, I still had a lot of the old mentality that nothing good could happen for blacks in Simpson County, and if it did, it couldn't last. If someone had told me in 1971 that in less than fifteen years we'd have a recreation center, a youth program, a health clinic, adult education classes, a farm, a housing program, a law clinic, a full grade school, and other programs, I'd have said, "No way! You're crazy!"

But as I stood there in front of that crowd, I suddenly realized: *This is for real! I'm not dreaming! This vision is really happening!* And I was so overwhelmed at the awesomeness of it that for one of the few times in my life, I was at a loss for words. I couldn't even finish my speech.

That was OK. It wasn't a day for speeches but for celebration! We finished off the program in the gym and then marched in a long line down to the new building. There we cut a ribbon and opened the facility for tours and refreshments. It was the greatest day I'd ever seen in Mendenhall.

When classes began, 105 children enrolled. The next year, when we added sixth grade, enrollment was up to 130.

Other numbers besides enrollment impressed us. Standardized test scores showed our students were performing exceptionally well. We also found a marked difference between them and transfer students, especially in reading. And when they moved to other parts of the country, they usually were ahead of their peers. Even in states like Massachusetts and California, which have some of the best schools in the country, our students were often advanced a grade. We weren't surprised when we started receiving high praise for the program from parents, educators, ministers, and others.

One day I chatted with Judi Adams. A lot had happened since she'd asked me what the outlook was for a Genesis One primary school. Now she was the administrator with lots of problems to solve. "Some days it's an uphill battle," she said with a sigh. "In fact, with some of these kids it seems like an impossible task. But just about the time we get discouraged, it seems like God shows us a glimpse of growth from a seed we've planted."

I liked the idea of comparing the school's work to planting seeds in young lives. It fit with the rural flavor of our town. I felt like a farmer trying to provide all the right conditions for plants to spring up. Now it was up to the kids themselves to make an effort to grow. And it was up to God to help them along.

Now as I walked past the school building each day, I thanked God for His answer to my prayers. One thing was for sure—He had caused it to happen, not me! Now I began praying a new prayer: *Lord, make these children into something! Make them lawyers and doctors, scientists and professors, businessmen and ministers, homemakers and missionaries!* And the more I thought about what these kids could become, I decided to throw in another "impossible" dream: *And Lord*, I added, *why not make one of them a President!*

THIRTEEN

HELP FOR THE BODY,

HOPE FOR THE SOUL

Our ministry in Mendenhall matured and expanded, but outsiders had a hard time defining just what we were. To some we looked like a church, to others a community development organization. Which one was it? Even *we* got a bit confused at times. But one thing we never got confused about was our mission: trying to live out the gospel as a body of Christians. As long as we stayed focused on that, we weren't too concerned with what form our work took—or with what it looked like.

For a while there was confusion because we had no identifiable pastor in our fellowship. When John Perkins had directed the ministry, he fulfilled many pastoral functions—preaching and teaching, visiting sick folks, counseling, and so forth. Yet he never really viewed himself as a pastor. Nor did I view my work as that of a pastor when I returned in 1971. So when Rev. Artis Fletcher returned to the community in 1974 to serve as the pastor of Mendenhall Bible Church, we all felt that he would be meeting a critical need.

Artis and I had worked together as students in John's ministry during summers. After high school he had attended Washington Bible College before taking a church in Maryland. Later he completed his degree at LABC. Along with a pastor's heart, Artis brought know-how in carpentry, plumbing, electrical

work, and automotive repair. Better yet, he brought a willingness to use these skills to help people.

In coming back to Simpson County he was also providing a
homecoming for Carolyn, his wife—the same Carolyn Albritton
who had brought Rosie to the ministry in Mendenhall and had
been among the first black female students at LABC.

Along with my old friend, Jimmie Walker, Artis and I formed
a second-generation team to carry on the ministry that John
Perkins had started. As soon as he settled in, we talked about
plans for Mendenhall Bible Church. "Artis, you know this is a
heavily churched area. We've got all kinds of churches around
here. Some people complain that churches are too emotional,
others say they're not emotional enough. Some folks want the
church to just stick to preaching the gospel and not mess with
social concerns. But others say just the opposite. I know you'll
preach the gospel. But what else do you have in mind for the
program at Mendenhall Bible Church?"

His response showed a wisdom beyond his years. "Is there
any reason why we can't do evangelism, teach the Word of God,
and help people with their social needs? These are all jobs that
belong to the body of Christ. I look at what you're doing in all
the ministries you've got going, and I believe they should be a
part of every church's outreach."

"Then why don't we consider our present ministries and any
we add in the future as arms of Mendenhall Bible Church?"

Artis liked that idea. "The way I see it, they naturally flow out
of what we've traditionally called missions."

In this way Artis and I built a strong commitment to the
work in Mendenhall and to each other. As pastor of Mendenhall Bible Church, his focus would be on preaching the
gospel and nurturing a body of Christians who were becoming
more committed to living out that gospel, especially as it spoke
to the responsibility of Christians to the poor. I would be the
executive director of the various ministries that expressed
what living out the gospel meant.

This commitment to a common vision was easy for Artis and
me to talk about. But it was harder to explain to others. And it
was harder still to maintain in the day-to-day work of the
church and the outreach ministries. We wanted all of our workers—the medical staff, teachers, youth workers, office person-

nel—to carry out their assignments with Christlike concern. Our fear was that they would lose sight of the underlying spiritual basis. So at one point we encouraged them to identify people who needed counseling for spiritual and other kinds of problems and refer them to Artis or me.

This was well-intentioned. But in time it led to a misperception. People began to think that Mendenhall Bible Church was the only place for evangelism and discipleship. The outreach ministries, on the other hand, were responsible for carrying out services like health care, education, and housing. So when someone raised a spiritual issue, our workers would say, "Oh, go over to the church if you want to know more about that. That's their job. I'm just a teacher" (or a nurse, or a secretary, or whatever).

When we discovered this confusion, we had to review our common mission with everyone involved. In fact, we've continued to evaluate who we are as a ministry every two years. It's so easy to get off base. And what gets lost sight of first is the spiritual. What stays is the concern for social problems because they're so easy to see and the results are sooner in coming.

But what we want is for every worker to do his work out of a spirit of Christlike service. And we want every one of them to know how to lead someone to Jesus Christ and to actually see that task of evangelism as a part of his job.

The spiritual and the social—both are so important, and so related. I'm often asked how we balance these in our ministries. Usually folks want to concentrate on one or the other: "How many have been saved?" they'll ask. Others want to know, "How much money have you put toward housing? What sorts of grants have you received?"

My answer is always the same: We want to meet the needs of both Christians and non-Christians, black or white, whatever those needs are, to the extent that we can. Presenting the gospel is always a priority for us, but we never ignore other needs. In fact, unless we show Christian love and concern in dealing with some of the desperate physical needs that people have, such as hunger or illness, they can't hear us when we talk about spiritual things.

Why the priority on the gospel? Because as important as economic and social development are, those alone are not enough. Without changed hearts, both black people and white

125

people are ultimately lost and alone in dealing with the ultimate problem—sin. Only Jesus can deal with that. Yet the gospel doesn't end with a person praying to receive Christ's salvation. It must go on into living with biblical values and with showing compassion for all needs of people. Our emphasis is not just the gospel or just social concern, but both—not either/or, but both/and.

Artis often preached along these lines. One Sunday he was especially eloquent: "If we have political success and we have economic success but don't have Christian values, we'll become oppressors," he told us. "For years blacks have pointed their fingers at whites and said, 'You're unjust! You're unfair!' Yet they have a tendency to do exactly the same thing if they get some power. They oppress whites as well as their own people. They don't have the commitment or the heart to use their advancement or their resources to make life better for people in their communities."

Then he added an illustration that drove the point home. "One time I visited a man in Los Angeles. He lived in one of those big apartment houses subsidized by the government—the kind with people piled on top of people. He complained to me, 'I'm in the ghetto! They won't let me up! I can't get no job! I can't take care of my family! They're keeping me down!' At the time he was saying all this, he was going to trade school.

"Later I visited him again. Only now he was successful in his trade—so successful that he had his own business and was making $400 to $500 a day, really big money for him. You know what he said to me this time? He told me, 'Artis, black people in the ghetto are lazy! They just won't work!'"

The congregation laughed nervously, but you could feel everyone's anger at the man's comment. Artis went on. "Once he made it out of the ghetto, he bought himself a home in a nicer community, he put a fence around it, he bought a Cadillac—and three dogs to protect it! He's a good example of how economics alone is not the answer.

"You see, without Christian values, without the commitment to make life better for people in his community, without the commitment Christ had, all he wanted was to get what he wanted for himself. The first step in getting Christian values is to be reconciled to God through Christ. Then you let God direct your life because He knows what's best for you. He can enable you to be concerned about others, just as He is."

As Artis spoke, I felt personally challenged. I recalled those years when I desperately wanted to get out of Mississippi. Even after I'd been reconciled to God, even after college and seminary when God was turning me homeward, I tried to ignore Him in a way. I'd never lost my compassion for the poor. But I had no intention of returning to the place I'd tried so hard to get away from. I even had many legitimate reasons not to return. Like the man in the story, I'd felt the strong appeal of upward mobility.

My feelings toward Southern whites were a problem, too. I held onto memories of my bad experiences with them, but I forgot the good ones. I knew God wanted me to seek reconciliation with white people in Mendenhall. But I was struggling with memories of being cheated as a sharecropper, of Mama's lynching stories, and of John's beatings.

Suddenly I realized that Artis was speaking to this very point. "Having Christian values means being reconciled to our fellowman. The unreconciled man, even though he may be a Christian, is on an ego trip. He's got to be up here"—Artis raised his hand up high—"while his fellowman is down here"—he pointed down to the floor. "He's gotta have power. He's gotta see himself as being greater. And that's where the oppression comes in.

"But if I want to be reconciled to someone, I've got to see that I'm no better than he is. I've got to be willing to commit myself to helping him. I might have more money than he does, or more education. But that doesn't put me above him. Being reconciled to God, myself, and to my fellowman makes me committed to helping him — in his poverty, in his habitual drunken state, in his marital or home problems, in keeping a job. I commit myself to helping him become a total man. I commit myself to using my resources to help him—even my economic power, if I have any. I know that God wants to make life better for both of us because He loves us."

Artis's sermon encouraged me and troubled me all at the same time. I thought about how crucial commitment and showing God's love were in our various ministries. I was excited to see oppressed people "bloom" as a result of our work. But I saw little reconciliation with our white neighbors, and that bothered me a lot. I realized that I myself had not dealt with the pain I'd grown up with in a segregated society. There was still some bitterness alive, deep down inside me. God was telling me to deal with it. He wanted me to seek reconciliation with the one type of person I most detested—the Southern white.

F O U R T E E N

THE ROAD

TO RECONCILING

THE RACES

"Someone's talkin' about shootin' up your house!" the caller told me. "Artis Fletcher's, too!"

A chill raced through me as I set down the phone. Was this just a prank? I decided to find out. I began contacting various leaders in the community and learned that others had gotten wind that something was up. "You better watch out!" one warned. "I know who's behind all this. They've hired a black man to kill you!"

I didn't take that as idle gossip. That sort of thing had been done before. In fact, it had happened to Martin Luther King. A woman walked up to him and asked, "Are you Martin Luther King?" When he said yes, she stabbed him with an ice pick. It came so close to his heart that if he had sneezed, he would have died.

So I got on the phone with Artis and discussed the situation. We could see some reasons why we might be targets. We'd been aggressively challenging some evils in the community. Maybe our opponents wanted to scare us into silence. Then, too, elections were coming up in the county, and we had publicly backed some black candidates along with some white candidates we felt would look after the interests of both blacks and whites.

To make matters worse, the Ku Klux Klan had started marching in Mendenhall, both hooded and unhooded. It was the first time ever that I could recall such boldness on their part. Normally they would wear hoods and thus be more or less anonymous. But now they were openly defying black civil rights. And this was in July of 1979!

I wondered: *Are we going back to the forties and fifties? Can something like this really happen, with all the litigation locally by John Perkins, and all the legislation nationally by Congress, and all the pressure for change brought on by the civil rights movement? Is all that going to amount to nothing?*

Later the police called both Artis and me to say that threats had been made against us. They never identified the source of their information.

So something was up. But what did it all mean? I wasn't afraid of a white person driving into the "black quarters" and shooting into my house. But this sounded like a white person paying a black to threaten me and my family. That was very frightening. I didn't know from what direction the violence might come. Who should I trust? And when would it happen? Tonight? Tomorrow night? Next week? There was no telling.

I had to take the threat seriously and protect my family. As dusk approached, our neighbors volunteered to stay up that night in shifts to keep a lookout. It was comforting to feel their support.

Meanwhile, at the insistence of my neighbor, I got out a hunting rifle that I'd recently bought. When he saw it, he declared, "That li'l ole rifle ain't gonna stop nothin'!" He went home and came back with a massive shotgun. "You use this and you be safe!" he promised.

"Get that shotgun outta here!" I replied with a laugh. "I don't need that!"

We put Danita, now age five, and Reggie, now two, to bed in our bedroom. We also had guests in from Oregon, two white folks, and we offered to make other arrangements for them. But they chose to stay and place themselves at risk and suffer with us. In fact, they even ignored our suggestion to put their mattresses on the floor.

The night passed without incident. But we stayed on our guard for several nights. Finally, though, we decided that we couldn't let this situation dominate our lives. We'd just have to trust God to take care of us. So we went back to our normal sleeping arrangements.

Nothing ever came of the threats. Artis and I continued to speak out on social and political issues, as well as spiritual ones. The elections came and went. The Klan went about their business. And life went on. I never did find out the whole story.

But one thing I realized was that I needed to think long and hard about my own attitude toward whites. I'd grown up in a system where, as a black person, I was a second-class citizen. My response to that had been an attempt to leave Mississippi and never come back. But that response only took me away from the problem; it didn't deal with the problem. The problem was racism. And I hated to see it in whites.

But what I came to see was that I had racist attitudes myself. I wasn't in a position to demonstrate my racism the way that whites were. When I'd been laying sewer pipe in Anguilla, the white boss had cursed me and made my life miserable. He was in control, so he was able to do that. His racism came out in very visible ways. Mine came out more subtly. One of the most apparent was that I'd write off all whites, at least all Southern whites. As soon as I heard a Southern drawl, I'd say to myself, *I'm not going to listen to this person. He's a white Southerner. He's a racist.*

It was interesting, though, how God used that attitude to humble me. I spoke once at the University of Illinois. Afterward a man came up and said, "I'm from Mississippi, too. Now I'm a Southern Baptist pastor here." He was white. He had a noticeable Southern drawl. He was a Southern Baptist preacher. I stereotyped him immediately: Racist!

But just before I completely tuned him out I heard the words, "I'm really concerned about people." That one statement kept me listening. The longer he talked, the more I realized that behind his Southern ways this man was not just a religious person, but a spiritual person. He wasn't someone who was letting racism dictate his faith. Instead, his faith dictated a deep concern for reconciliation and a passion to see people, black or white, come to know Christ as their Savior. I'd misjudged him. I think I even apologized to him, even though he hadn't known what was going through my mind.

That incident, more than any other, showed me that I needed to be quiet and listen and not be so quick to stereotype. Yes, racism was deeply rooted and widespread in the South. But the place to start stamping it out was in me. I needed to surrender my own biased attitudes and actions to God first, then let Him go to work to change the rest of society.

I remember preaching once in one of the largest churches in California. My theme was loving your neighbor. Afterward, a white woman came up to meet me. She was blind. "I want to give my life to Christ as a result of what you said today," she explained. I learned that she had spent most of her life in Mississippi. Yet here she was in California, asking for spiritual help from a black man! I felt stunned. God had brought us both thousands of miles in order to "cross the tracks" and talk! She was reconciled to God that day. And I took a giant step forward in my own reconciliation toward Southern whites.

But not every encounter went so well. In several churches in Jackson, I wasn't allowed to speak because of my race. I felt so bitter! God used a group called Faith at Work to break down some barriers there. As pioneers in the small group movement, Faith at Work was invited to come to Jackson and hold a conference. They told the churches that they would hold the conference only if the meetings were integrated and if blacks could be involved in the planning. That was a big risk for Faith at Work to take. But they believed God would bring about racial reconciliation in response to their faith.

The conference went forward, and I was asked to participate. In one of my workshops I had an all-white group, and there I met a man named Guy Parker. Guy had grown up in Mississippi; he knew blacks were treated differently and saw it as a fact of life. But God began to work in his life at that conference. His strong, strict racism began to dissolve as he listened and considered the truth of God's Word. In time he experienced a complete reversal in his attitude toward blacks, even risking his reputation and relationships to other whites. But he didn't mind. He knew he could no longer stand by, knowing it was wrong and doing nothing about it. Through that experience he became a dear friend and eventually a member of our ministry's board. He's a clear model of the grace of God—a racist saved by grace!

As a result of such experiences, I began to learn some strategies for breaking down racial barriers. Reconciliation involves more than just getting whites and blacks to live and work side by side. It means accepting each other as human beings made in the image of God. It also involves an active concern for the welfare of each other.

The place to begin is with vulnerability. If folks from different races really want to communicate with each other, they've got to be honest and genuine. Blacks, for example, often need to take the initiative to ask questions, to discuss issues, to show concern. Perhaps the habit of deferring to whites has made us afraid to speak up. As a result, we too often hang back and appear silent or disinterested. I recall how the death of Martin Luther King prompted me to start making myself heard and known at LABC. Once I did, I found a whole new set of relationships with the white students. We got into some great discussions in which a lot of misinformation and misunderstandings got cleared up and new ideas got formed.

Whites, on the other hand, often seem to float right by black people as if they don't exist or don't matter. Perhaps they're afraid of getting involved or getting hurt. But reconciliation can't occur unless we risk ourselves with others. I think of Chris Erb and her devotion to the children of Simpson County. She didn't have to come here. She could have stayed in her very comfortable background in Pennsylvania. But she made a permanent difference in the lives of countless children because she refused to ignore the plight of blacks when she heard about it.

Another way to break down barriers is to develop common meeting places. This has already happened through the public schools. But one place it hasn't happened very much is in the church. By and large we still have segregated churches. For that matter, we still have segregated communities. As a result, we're not around persons from other races and backgrounds enough to know what life is like for them. It's easy to ignore them—and to misunderstand them. At Mendenhall Bible Church we have a predominantly black congregation. But there are a few whites, plus frequent white visitors. That has helped all of us to get to know each other in a way that respects racial differences yet overlooks them enough to treat each other as people with dignity.

That brings up a third strategy: We need to get to know somebody who is the object of our racism. If I'm black, I need to get to know someone who is white, not so that I can tell people I have a white friend, but so that I can learn more about whites—and about my attitudes toward whites. That's where growth takes place. That was the great value in having a white roommate at LABC. For the first time in my life, I had to get to know someone who was white. I was scared. I had some funny ideas about what might happen. I made plenty of mistakes. But I also benefited as I saw some of my own prejudices and weaknesses.

A related idea is churches having someone in their pulpit periodically who is the object of their racism. An all-white suburban church needs to have a black person preach sometimes, and vice versa. That affirms something important: It shows everyone that this person is all right, that he has something to say to us that we need to hear. For some churches that may sound like a radical step. But we need to become aggressive to do something, rather than to remain passive, doing nothing.

A final way to break down barriers is to get involved in helping people that we wouldn't ordinarily help. That's hard. I know that when needy people come my way, I feel myself sighing, "Oh, why do you have to ask me for help? I'm so busy! I'm already doing so much! Now this needy person wants more from me." My agenda just doesn't allow for anybody else to intrude.

But at that moment I have to remind myself that needy people will always be the last to get some consideration. I know, because when I was a boy, I came from a needy family. Nobody seemed to care whether we lived or died. In fact, I sometimes got the feeling that some folks would rather we just died! Praise God for the lady who gave me Bible verses to memorize so I could go to camp! Praise God for John Perkins so that I could find assurance of my salvation and start growing as a Christian! Praise God for David Nicholas and John MacArthur who invited me to apply for a scholarship to LABC! People like these changed my life because they were willing to move the needy up in their agenda.

Reconciliation between blacks and whites is not easy to bring about. After so many ugly years of racial mistrust and hatred, it's hard to talk, much less cooperate. But God calls us to make the effort. So our choices in this area boil down to a question of obedience. Are we going to do what God says and be reconciled to our neighbor, no matter what color his skin is? Or are we going to ignore God and hold onto attitudes of prejudice and bigotry? I want to choose the path of obedience to God. For me that has meant learning to avoid stereotyping whites and instead reaching out with compassion in whatever way I can.

That doesn't mean, of course, letting people do whatever they please. There's a place for self-protection. God is a God of justice, and He wants the rights of poor people to be respected. That's why early in the work I sought to bring a government-sponsored legal services office to our community. When the service was approved, Central Mississippi Legal Services opened in our former health clinic building. Now our community had legal help right on our doorstep.

The staff included a lawyer, a paralegal, and a secretary. The lawyer assigned was Suzanne Griggins, a white woman from Illinois. We got to know her as we worked together helping poor people. She played on our softball team and attended Mendenhall Bible Church from time to time.

One day Suzanne asked to meet with Artis. She told him she'd been brought up in a Roman Catholic family but had turned away from religion in college. She considered herself an atheist. But after listening to some of Artis's sermons and observing our work, she had some questions. She was curious about Christianity and what motivated our staff. Why were we so dedicated to helping people? And why did we try to tie our faith into everything we did?

With Bible in hand, Artis answered her questions one by one. He also explained the way of salvation. This led to a series of conversations. Then one day he told her that he thought it was time for her to decide what she would do about the gospel. She replied that she was ready to become a Christian.

Soon afterward, we received word that the government planned to close Suzanne's office due to budget cuts under the Reagan administration. We were devastated. Who would help poor people with their legal needs now? Where could we find the money to replace what we had? Should we even try to operate a legal clinic as part of our ministry?

I talked about it with Suzanne. "We've watched your work for several years now. Nobody doubts your commitment to the poor. But I'm wondering: As a Christian, would you be willing to make a commitment to our ministry and continue your work as a member of our staff?"

"Dolphus," she said, "I remember becoming so irritated when people called the legal services office and asked, 'Is this the ministry lawyer?' I hated it when people associated me with a Christian ministry. I sometimes wished our office was anywhere but here, next to you and your ministries. But as I watched and listened, I began to admire the way you do things. I've come to respect you a lot—the way you stand up for change and people's rights. But at the same time you show love and patience, even to those who treat you badly."

Is that a yes or a no? I wondered.

"I don't think that I understand yet all that's involved in a Christian approach to legal services," she told me, "but if you're willing, I'm willing to stay and learn."

Everyone was overjoyed! At great sacrifice, her commitment enabled us to continue offering legal services from a Christian perspective to poor folks for miles around. We called her new ministry the Community Law Office (CLO) and used it to reach out to Christians and non-Christians alike.

One of the principles that Suzanne instituted was exhausting every possibility of negotiating legal settlements outside of court. One time, for example, two black high school coaches were fired from their jobs. Various reasons were given for their dismissal. One was charged with failing to teach the fundamentals of basketball and failing to recruit students to play ball. The other had similar charges. However, both were next in line to become athletic directors. In fact, one had eighteen years of experience and had been named Coach of the Year three times.

They wanted to file a job discrimination suit. But first Suzanne requested a hearing with the schools on their behalf. When it was over, she burst into my office. "Both coaches were reinstated!" she exclaimed proudly. "I thought we'd never reach an agreement. It took twelve hours! But the outcome was worth it." I admired Suzanne for handling the situation the way she did. It must have been hard for her not to lash out in anger in the face of deliberate discrimination. But she had come to see herself as a representative of Christ in her profession. She was just as interested in serving His interests as those of her clients or the ministry's.

Sometimes, of course, negotiations failed and litigation was necessary. One of the larger cases involved zoning of voter districts. For years an at-large manner of voting made it virtually impossible for a black to be elected to the board of aldermen, depriving us of representation. We tried every way possible to make things more equitable. But in the end, the CLO filed a suit against the city, trying to get it to abolish the at-large system and replace it with a plan that divided the city into five wards, with one of the wards predominantly black. Our plan was adopted, so now we have a black alderman.

Many Christians seem to shy away from taking legal action, as if Christ wouldn't approve. But we've learned that the economic, educational, and social justice that God desires for people doesn't just happen. We have to work for it. Sometimes that can happen through negotiations and coming up with creative alternatives. But sometimes it takes aggressive litigation to protect the rights of people.

The best things happen, though, when blacks and whites work together to resolve differences and solve problems. Not long ago a vote came up on whether Mendenhall should allow the sale of alcohol. The town had always been dry, and we felt that that had been a positive influence on the community. So when some white leaders in town invited Artis and me to a meeting to stop the legalization effort, we showed up. It was a good discussion in which we came up with a solid strategy, one that helped to defeat the proposal.

One of the best ways we've found of enlisting whites in our work and of sharing what we've learned with them is through a number of internships in our various programs. We've had students come from nearby Mississippi College and from as far away as Harvard and Stanford.

Word got around about the unique legal internship offered by the law office, so we were never surprised by the inquiries that came—never, that is, until one day Suzanne told me, "Dolphus, I received a letter today from an organization that wants to send a law student from South Africa."

"South Africa!" I said, feeling a mixture of surprise and suspicion. "Is he black?"

"No, he's white."

I thought she was joking, but then I realized she was serious. "I don't know, Suzanne. We'd better think about this. What's the organization?"

"It's called the Student's Cross-cultural Missions Program, SCAMP. They want to send him to us as a student delegate."

I read the letter. This group had apparently sent a delegate to the Voice of Calvary ministry in Jackson the year before. That person had picked up some literature about our ministry and taken it back to South Africa. As a result, a student named Carl wanted to come to Mendenhall.

Suzanne and I had a lot of questions we wanted answered before making a decision. Where did this group stand on apartheid? Was Carl concerned for helping oppressed people? Would he take what he learned and apply it in his own country? Could he relate well to our black community? Or would he alienate them?

For weeks we talked and prayed and tried to find out more about this organization called SCAMP. Not wanting to misjudge them, we asked them to give us information about their purpose and programs. Their mission, they explained, was to train people to carry out the greater mission of Christ. They also raised a legitimate question on their student's behalf: How would blacks in the Mendenhall area treat a South African student?

Finally Suzanne gave me a vision for what this opportunity could mean. "Wouldn't it be exciting if we could help in even a small way to equip someone to be an influence for good in South Africa?"

Her words electrified me. Exciting? No, it would be incredible! Right away we wrote an approval for the internship.

Seven months later, Carl arrived by bus from New York City. From the start he showed an attitude of serving and learning. He was open about his government—and concerned about it, too. Suzanne reported that he was fitting in really well. "The Lord has sent us someone very special," she told me.

I agreed. Best of all, He was doing something very special with our work. The ripples of hope that we'd created were now expanding outside the community, across the country, and even around the world. I wondered how far they could reach.

138

FIFTEEN

KEEPING

THE FLAME BURNING—

AND SPREADING

One hot, humid Sunday afternoon in 1982, three white men arrived in Mendenhall. Wayne Gordon, a pastor from Chicago, and two members of his congregation had been attending a conference on ministry to the poor, sponsored by Voice of Calvary in Jackson. "We've been going to workshops and listening to speeches about 'holistic' ministries to needy people," Wayne explained. "And we keep hearing about your work here as a model of that. So we decided to come see for ourselves."

For three hours they fired questions at me, and I explained our philosophy and the workings of Mendenhall Ministries. I also learned that they had a vision, too. When Wayne had been a senior at Wheaton College in Wheaton, Illinois, he had determined to develop a ministry to people in the inner city of Chicago.

"After I graduated I moved to the Lawndale neighborhood in Chicago and worked with the Fellowship of Christian Athletes coaching football. I got to know youth in the area, and some of them gave their lives to the Lord. Then their parents became Christians, and soon we had the nucleus of a church, which we named Lawndale Community Church.

"Dolphus, our people are a lot like the folks here in Simpson County, only they live in a huge city. But they lack adequate health care and other services, and they're very poor. We'd like to begin a holistic ministry similar to yours. Will you help us get started?"

I felt honored by the request. But I had a question to ask them. "Tell me, are you willing to commit to a ministry like that over a long period of time?"

"I've already made that commitment," Wayne replied. "I moved to the inner city eight years ago. My house has been broken into at least a dozen times. But I still have a deep love for the people. Despite the struggles and the risks, I've determined to stay. I wonder, though, can a white person be effective trying to minister to blacks?"

I could see the determination in his eyes and his deep concern for the people in his community. He'd obviously paid his dues and was now looking for a way to get things going. "If you're willing to commit yourself to a long-term ministry and to live in the neighborhood, I don't think you'll have any problem," I told him. Before he left, I agreed to visit Lawndale and talk to the people in his church.

I was thrilled about Mendenhall Ministries serving as a model for Wayne's group. For some time we had been praying that others would catch a vision for ministering to meet the whole range of needs that poor people have.

So in the fall I traveled to Lawndale to speak and show a film about our work. Lawndale Community Church operated out of a storefront deep in the city. As I talked with the people and observed their programs, I could tell that this group meant business. The same heart for the poor that Wayne had displayed was evident in the others, too.

The next summer, Wayne brought a larger group to Mendenhall, made up of key people in the church. He also invited me to serve on their board.

In the fall I returned to Lawndale to lead a seminar on how they could develop ministries to meet people's needs. Since they were already committed to such a ministry, my purpose was to help them decide where to begin, and to share what we'd learned from our experience.

"At Mendenhall," I explained, "we started with the belief that all things are possible through Christ. That was vital because we recognized years ago that our vision to serve the people in our area was far beyond our means. We couldn't do everything. We couldn't begin to meet all of the needs we saw.

"So over the years our vision has become to connect with resources and skills outside our community, so that some of the needs inside our community could be met. We've tried to identify Christians with skills in a particular area and then put them in touch with the people who need to see God's love in action in that area."

Did that mean that we only developed programs if we could find volunteers and others to provide skills and resources? How did we know which programs to get started on?

"In moving ahead we always have to reckon with both human and divine factors. Faith and practicality aren't opposites—they're partners. I like to say it this way: Faith is realism that takes God into account in our plans and visions. Faith doesn't send us charging into every possible ministry, recklessly squandering financial and human resources. We're not a grocery shopper, merrily filling a cart, expecting God to pay the bill.

"Instead, each time we face an opportunity for a new ministry, we ask: Is this a true felt need in the broader community, or is it just a perceived need from our perspective? Do our people share the vision? Is there leadership within the local Christian community who will commit themselves to a long-term process of seeing this vision materialize? And do we have the necessary economic resources?"

I explained that the stability of a program depends on having the right leadership, a solid economic base, and a realistic five-year plan. We discussed their ideas for Lawndale, and I asked them: Who is your target group? What specific services do you plan to provide? How will you organize to get the job done? Who is your leadership? Who raises the money? How? Who makes spending decisions? How will you network with other churches?

I pointed out that Mendenhall Ministries is an outreach of Mendenhall Bible Church. We think of ourselves as a body of Christians glorifying Christ by mobilizing human resources as well as economic, legal, educational, and physical resources, from a biblical perspective, to produce a better quality of life for our area. I encouraged them to tie their work into the Lawndale Community Church in a similar way.

As we considered these areas, the group decided that a health clinic should be a priority. After I left, they moved ahead and eventually launched one. Later they opened a thrift store and a recreation center. The parallels to Mendenhall were clear.

But it was not only in Chicago that our work in rural Simpson County began to have an influence. Christians in Denver, Seattle, Washington, D.C., Poughkeepsie (New York), Macon (Mississippi), and several other cities also approached me about learning from our ministry. In Dallas, Sayers and Kathy Dudley, a white couple, caught a vision for reaching out to some of that city's poorest citizens near the projects in west Dallas. I was privileged to help them launch Voice of Hope Ministries, and today it's a growing, vital force for Christian ministry in that community.

It's exciting to see that kind of impact. But it also forces me to ask, What is it that folks are hearing about us? What is it that they're coming to see? Do we really have anything to show them? I worry sometimes that we can expand what we're doing and show it off to people, but it might not have much stability or depth. We're in our second generation of leadership, and I often think of a proverb: The first generation has the vision and lays a foundation; the second generation lives off the reputation of the first generation; and the third generation comes and sells everything. I don't want that!

Consequently, in recent years I've been eager to prune back less productive work in order to build strength and stability into what we're doing well. We're still interested in growing. But growth does not necessarily mean expansion. If we're too weak to handle the programs we do have, we have no business adding new ones. We want our ministry to become a model for Christian outreach in the truest sense of the word—not something that sounds great from a distance but is a disappointment when you actually see it.

Two areas in which we've had to learn some hard lessons along these lines have been volunteers and funding. Volunteers have been critical to our work. Without them we couldn't have held our original tutoring program, built the multipurpose center and Genesis One School, staffed our housing program, or carried out most of our other ministries. In fact, they've been so important to our efforts that I used to worry that we were exploiting them.

But then I discovered that in a way we were letting them exploit us! Well-meaning people would come in to help for a few days or for a summer, and we needed their skills and energy. But sometimes we spent more time and effort managing and attending to them than we did helping the local people who we are here to serve. Even our own staff sometimes felt less important or unneeded. Sometimes volunteers ended up doing most of the work, while the local crowd stood back, awed by their technical skills and feeling inferior because of their own lack of expertise.

Volunteers have also tended to work with more enthusiasm than local people, perhaps because the project is new to them and they're there because they want to help people. They also know that theirs is a short-term commitment, so they don't get as tired of the task the way those of us who live here tend to do. And knowing that they'll be going home soon, they don't have to deal with the long-term, chronic problems that defy an easy solution.

This short-term involvement has sometimes led us into taking on work that we can't support once the volunteer leaves. Outsiders will come in and see needs and then suggest all kinds of ideas, most of them excellent, for meeting those needs. In the early days we would launch a program based on such ideas, and the volunteer would help us get things started. But then he would leave, and we'd suddenly realize that we were left to keep the program going without his support. That produced a lot of weak programs—and an overworked staff!

Most of our outside volunteers have been white. Sometimes the black people trying to work with them have felt inadequate, especially if the white person was aggressive and assertive. This was counterproductive. By flooding our small black community with white volunteers, we were taking away experience from the local folks we wanted to develop. So at one point we had to decline the help of volunteers until we could work out a more balanced program. I told our workers, "If we don't do it, nobody's going to do it!" That helped to reawaken their motivation and creativity, and they recaptured ownership of the vision.

Not everyone can come to Mendenhall as a volunteer, so many people have sent their money instead. This, too, has been invaluable in making the dream possible. Black Mendenhall has very few stores or businesses. We don't yet have economic systems plowing profits back into the local community. So we depend a lot on outsiders with resources to fund our work.

Yet here, too, we've learned some important lessons. Fund-raising is a sensitive area for most people, but especially for me. Even though I grew up poor, I've always been a hard worker. So at first, the thought of asking people for money felt like begging. I'd also heard white folks make remarks about blacks being lazy. Well, I wasn't lazy! In fact, I spent the first half of my life going to college and seminary and graduate school, trying to prove to everybody that I wasn't. Somehow asking people for money seemed to recall that stereotype, and it hurt.

So I had a lot to overcome when I started raising the ministry's funds. In time I learned that people wanted to give. But they wanted to give to people, not to programs. They wanted to invest in people who were faithfully carrying out God's work in an effective way. So my focus shifted from a concern over being thought lazy to a concern for being found faithful. That helped a lot.

I also had to learn that just because someone wants to fund an idea for a program, that doesn't necessarily mean that we should start that program. Funding has always been an important consideration. But the real question we've had to answer is, Is this a need that God wants us to meet, right now, in the way that's been suggested? Our board has become so helpful in answering this question. They've realized how easily donors can dictate the direction of the ministry. They've also reminded me that donors don't have to live with the consequences of funding decisions.

One problem I've occasionally encountered in fund-raising is an attitude of despair. People will hear about Simpson County and perhaps come visit us. They'll see sights of extreme poverty, such as folks living in shacks with dirt floors and no electricity. And instead of feeling compassion and asking God how they could help, they just say, "It's hopeless! There's nothing anyone can do about it! Nothing's going to change!"

When I hear that I think, *How ironic! That's the same attitude I had when I was living in a shack. I thought it was hopeless, too. Yet here I am seeing God work incredible changes in just a few years.*

I also think that such despair reflects a worldly perspective, not a godly one. The world looks at massive problems and says they're too great, they can't be solved, so the best anyone can do is take care of himself and his family and not try to save the world. But that's a selfish and defeatist perspective. Maybe we can't save the world. Maybe we can't save all of Simpson County. But we can help one person here—maybe one child in the Genesis One School, or one family that doesn't have any food, or one elderly person who needs a doctor.

I've been amazed at how the little tutorial program that Chris Erb was running when I came back in 1971 has grown into at least a dozen other ministries that have rescued countless people from poverty and hopelessness. God has taken the little ripples of hope that John Perkins started and multiplied them across the country, if not around the world. I recently attended a conference with people from at least thirty-five ministries that had taken inspiration and instruction from what has happened in Mendenhall.

It's always a mistake to look at a bad situation and say it's hopeless. With God, nothing is hopeless. When I left Mississippi for California it was because I thought nothing could ever change. But with God, all things are possible. So I came back, not because I thought I could change the situation, but because I believed that God could—and that He would if I'd be faithful to help the people He brought my way. I concentrated on what I could do instead of what I couldn't do. As a result, God has used me to bring forth impossible dreams and ripples of hope.

SIXTEEN

A VISION OF A

TRANSFORMED LIFE

"I feel like I'm alive again!" she told me. Looking into her eyes, I could believe it. They sparkled with enthusiasm. In fact, her whole posture communicated confidence. Though short and stout, the woman held her head up high and carried herself with dignity. As we chatted on the steps of the ministry's offices, I could hardly believe she was the same person who had come to me only a month or two earlier, defeated in spirit, hungry, and without anywhere to turn.

"Y'know, Dolphus, when I first met you I had no goal, no desire, nothin' to live for. Worst of all, I knew I was a sinner, but I didn't know what to do about it."

I said I knew that Artis had been counseling her. "Has that helped?"

Her face wrinkled up in a beaming smile. "Dolphus, I've come to God! For the first time in my life I got peace of mind!"

My heart exploded with joy, and I gave her a big hug. I felt I was welcoming someone into the family. I guess I was! "Have you told Marcella?" Marcella, a member of our staff, had been the first one to contact this woman about how we might help her.

"Not yet, but I'm fixin' to."

We talked about how she could grow spiritually, about how important it was that she stay involved in her Bible study group and the church fellowship. "I will!" she promised. "Those people really know how to love!"

"I hear your kids are doing well at Genesis One School," I said.

"Oh, yeah, they're so anxious to get there every day! They're not cryin' about food no more—just smilin'! They got a lot more energy, too."

"That's good! How are you getting along on that new job?"

"Oh, that's wonderful. I'm so glad to be back workin'. I hated welfare." She paused for a moment, and I could see she was looking back at some dark days. Finally she shook her head. "Y'know, nothin' seemed to work for me then. I was angry— angry at myself, angry at the world. When Marcella came, I didn't even want to believe that someone cared about listenin' to me. Things was so bad! Almost like there was no life left in me. There I was, on welfare, no husband, nobody to say, 'You can do somethin' with yourself! You can go on!' It's a good thing Marcella came along when she did."

"What did she say?"

"She told me about Mendenhall Ministries. She said I needed a place to learn about Christ and how to become the way God wanted me. She said there was a preacher here who really could help me feel like I wasn't alone. I don't know if I believed her, but I came anyway. What else was I gonna do? I didn't have no place else to go."

"So now you're glad you came?"

"I sure am! But you know, there's a lotta other folks out there who need to know somebody cares. They need help!"

"I know," I told her. "When I was growing up, my life was filled with a lot of things I hated. I became a Christian, too. And then through some other Christians God opened up a lot of doors for me to improve my life. Now I've got the privilege of doing something to help other people find better lives."

"Well, you sure helped me! Thank the Lord for you, Dolphus!"

I glowed inside as she went on her way. *Lord, it's all been worth it!* I sighed as I thought about how the various aspects of our work had combined to minister to this woman as a whole person. Along with Artis's counseling and spiritual nurture, we'd been able to assess her abilities and skills to see how she could best support her family. From the Thrift Store we'd gotten some clothing for her and her children, and a toaster oven to cook with. From the farm we supplied her with food and wood for her stove until she had found a job. The law office helped her get the child support that her former husband owed her. And her children were able to start coming to the Genesis One School.

This web of services had helped one woman and her family get started on the road back to purpose and productivity. It also got her started on the spiritual road of life in Christ.

But how many women must there be like her, not just in Simpson County, but across America? How many folks must there be who feel defeated, who face incredible needs, and who have nowhere to turn?

As a black person who came up out of grinding poverty, I'm particularly sensitive to conditions facing blacks today. Surveying the situation, I see a black America that, despite the gains of the civil rights movement, is in trouble socially, economically, but especially spiritually. The outlook for its youth is especially frightening. The black family is dissolving as the men take off, leaving the women to not only raise children but support them as well. There's a profound absence of strong male role models and leadership. Drug abuse is out of control, which means that crime is out of control. And too many of our people, especially our men, are wasting away in prison instead of living useful lives in the community.

There has been plenty of analysis trying to explain why all of this is true. But it hasn't produced much change. I believe that's because most of it fails to consider the critical importance of the spiritual element. Most efforts try to help poor people change their social status, economic status, educational status, legal status, and so on. These kinds of changes are important, which is why Mendenhall Ministries has the programs it does. But in order for real, lasting change to take place, we have to deal with people's hearts, with the spiritual dimension of their lives. We have to help them find a relationship with God. The gospel does that. It changes people from the inside out.

That's why I'm so happy when I see someone like the woman above. We helped her get on her feet financially and legally. We helped her children get the food and education they needed.

We helped her join a community of people where she could find support and friendships. But the most important thing we did for her, as she herself told me, is that we gave her the gospel. When God came into her life, her whole outlook changed. She came alive again.

So the gospel is not just an add-on for us. It's not something we do just because we're associated with a church. We believe it's the most important thing we offer, because it unleashes the power of God to change people's lives. Yes, we're concerned about people's physical and material circumstances. But we're also concerned about their spiritual circumstances. The challenge for us, as for anyone who works with the poor, is to bring these two aspects together.

Ironically, there was a time when churches could have addressed both these concerns and saved everyone a lot of heartache and a whole lot of dollars. In many inner city neighborhoods today, you'll see enormous old church buildings. A few still have little congregations struggling to hold on. But many are abandoned and boarded up. What happened was that when the neighborhoods began to change, the churches left the city and moved out to the suburbs where new homes were being built and higher income white folks were moving in.

Then in the late 1960s, the inner cities exploded. Suddenly the suburban church folks began to say, "Wow! We'd better go in there and do something! Let's fix the problems. Let's get people saved." But it was too late in most cases. Having left those people years before, it was almost impossible to come back and make much difference, now that poverty and racism and crime and drugs had taken over. The time to act would have been before those churches ever left the inner cities.

But that's water over the dam. Fortunately, God is raising up new works like Voice of Hope in Dallas and the Lawndale Community Church in Chicago. The great danger, though, is that white churches, hearing about such efforts, will say, "Thank God someone's doing something—so that we don't have to!" That would be a tragedy. No matter where one lives, he needs to rethink ministry in his own backyard. It's not just ministries overseas that deserve our attention, as important as those are. We also have to ask what God wants us to be doing ten miles away.

Acts 1:8 says that we should be proclaiming the gospel in Jerusalem, then in Judea, then in Samaria, and then to the remotest parts of the earth. Sometimes I think we've gotten so excited about reaching the remotest parts of the earth that we've neglected our own Jerusalem and Judea. But we have no business exporting a gospel to the peoples of Africa or Asia or South America that we've not been able to apply to the desperate needs of our own cities and towns.

One of my most important jobs at Mendenhall Ministries is to make sure our community is living out the gospel on our own doorstep. If we don't, our faith is nothing but a fantasy. If we do, our faith can produce miracles. In fact, one of the things that keeps me going is to see something that I thought was impossible come into being. It may be a changed individual, like that woman, or it may be an entire program, like the Genesis One School. When I walk into the Thrift Store and see blacks and whites shopping side by side, I think, *Can this be possible? Only a few years ago they wouldn't have even spoken to each other!* I walk into the law office and see black folks getting help from a white lawyer, and in the health clinic I see white folks getting help from a black doctor, and I think, *This is amazing! Right here in Simpson County something good is happening, despite racial differences. Praise God! Look what He's done! Look how far He's brought us!*

Of course, the job's not finished. There are still many, many needs to fill and people to help. We still need to build more homegrown leadership that understands the vision and can carry out the task. I'm anxious to see our young people go away from Simpson County to get the education and training they need and then return to pour their resources back into helping the community. We've already seen a number do that.

We also need to create a stable economic base. This means more than just generating outside dollars to keep things going. We desperately need those. But in the long term we need to develop local businesses owned and operated by black folks that will generate jobs and put money back into the community. A restaurant or small manufacturing plant could go a long way toward launching that vision.

There are many other resources we'd like to provide some-day. We need a counseling center where people can find help in dealing with some of their emotional and psychological needs. Years of poverty and racism have created enormous problems that must be solved if they're to become productive citizens. We also need to upgrade our housing program. Right now volunteers donate their skills to renovate run-down houses for folks who can't afford to fix them up. But this is still just a small effort.

Our volunteer program itself needs to grow beyond just bringing in people to do a little extra work. We need to make it a complete cross-cultural ministry experience, one in which visitors learn about the whole complex of poverty. We also need to develop training materials that will make our work more transferable. Right now, when someone contacts me to say they want to learn from what we're doing, we either have to go to them or bring them here, which takes time and energy away from our primary task in Mendenhall. We want our ministry to be a model, but we're still learning how to make that model transferable.

There is so much we'd like to do. But we're willing to wait for God. When He wants to make things happen, they'll happen. In the meantime, our job is to be faithful to do the best job we can on what He's given us today. I'm a great one for dreaming and seeing all the possibilities. I used to wonder if anything would ever happen here, or even could happen. Now, having seen God work miracles, I'm tempted to get a grocery list going of all the things I'd like to see Him do.

But that's not the way God works. Programs and successes are wonderful. Yes, but what matters is keeping our eyes on the Lord and depending on Him. That's why I want to give myself more and more to God's Word and prayer. I expect to be a part of this ministry and this community for many, many years, probably for the rest of my life. But I believe that the only way to sustain a lifetime of ministry like that is to maintain a growing walk with God.

When I was in Taiwan, God said to me, "Dolphus, you're black and I love you. You were born in the South, and I love you. Don't run away from your blackness or the fact that you're from the South. In Me you have security." That sense of God's love and approval gave me hope to return to Mississippi, and it's given me hope over the years when I've faced some very dark times. So as I look ahead to the coming years, that's where I want to put my confidence. Only God can sustain my hope. Only He can fulfill my deepest needs.

But I don't intend to just soak up God's goodness and forget about others. That's not the legacy I want to leave. When I was a boy, I never really had a father. I never had a man to look up to and say, "That's what I want to be like when I grow up." Somehow God brought along men who showed me the way. But when I think of what I'm passing on to Danita and Reggie and Ryan—and any other children God gives us—I want them to be able to say, "My dad had compassion for people. He loved people. He spent his life serving people—people that nobody else wanted to serve." To me, that's the kind of life that makes a difference. That's the kind of life that matters.

AFTERWORD BY WILLIAM HENDRICKS

This book began with Dolphus Weary falling into bed in a strange place, exhausted, a whirlwind of thoughts churning in his head. My own participation with Dolphus and his story began under similar circumstances. One night in the spring of 1986 I arrived in Mendenhall to produce a videotape for Mendenhall Ministries. As is often the case before I travel, I had slept fitfully the night before. So by the time I got to my room, I, like Dolphus in Taiwan, was ready to collapse into bed.

But also like Dolphus, sleep eluded me, that night, too. The Mississippi air was sultry, and no breeze seemed able to blow through the room, even though I'd thrown every window wide open. By midnight I managed to doze into a sweaty, half-conscious state. But somewhere around two-thirty or three, a dog yipped nearby.

It was like a spark touched to gunpowder. The night exploded in a melee of barking, howling, and growling. I think every dog in Simpson County had gathered outside, paying amorous court, I suppose, to some female canine. Eventually the mob trotted off, though I could still hear them away in the distance, tearing each other to pieces.

Now I was wide awake, and my mind kicked into gear. *Where am I?* I reflected. Mendenhall, of course. But where is Mendenhall? What is Mendenhall? What does this place mean? I realized how little I knew about this little hamlet that I was supposed to document on video. In fact, the main thing I knew about it was only how different it was in every way from Dallas, where I had grown up: rural, sleepy, quiet (except for dog fights!). I realized how unsettled I felt, how out-of-place.

I was staying in "the quarters," as black Mendenhall is referred to. What did that mean? I wasn't sure. I was white. I was an outsider. How would the black people respond to me? How would the whites? I'd heard lots of stories about Mendenhall,

155

the kind of stories related earlier in this book—troubling stories that made me wonder, *What am I doing here?*

Dolphus came to mind. I'd met Dolphus through a businessman who had seen my work and wanted me to produce a promotional tape for Mendenhall Ministries. I also knew about him from Gary Bauer, a fellow video producer and a member of the Mendenhall Ministries board. Gary had come with me to shoot the project. (Somehow he managed to sleep like a baby through all of this!)

Dolphus impressed me right off. I haven't known very many black people in my life. Of course, having grown up in Texas, I'd heard a lot of talk, both good and bad, about the way blacks and whites supposedly relate to each other. But such talk emphasized differences and ignored individual persons. Meeting Dolphus helped to remind me that when two people of a different race get to know each other, they can share a lot in common—and still respect each other's racial and cultural heritages.

Dolphus is a winsome, engaging person. It's easy to see why people in the Orient were drawn to him. I, too, felt warmed by his bright and ready smile, his firm, confident handshake, and his deep, booming voice. As I listened to him describe his work, I sensed a deep compassion for the poor, born out of a heart determined to honor God.

Still, as I tossed around in my damp sheets that night, I committed myself to professional detachment and skepticism. *Sure, Dolphus is a good guy,* I thought, *but can he be trusted? Is this Mendenhall Ministries for real, or is it just one more case of a charismatic leader using the plight of the poor to advance his own agenda?* Only time would tell. But I'd be watching.

As a video producer, I was in a good position to do so. I talked to everyone I could—staff, board members, volunteers, donors, insiders, outsiders, blacks, whites. Most important, I talked with folks on the receiving end of the ministry's efforts. "What has Mendenhall Ministries done for you?" I'd ask them.

Their answers were compelling. Time after time people told me about the practical, timely help they'd received. Some told stories of simple acts of kindness, others testified to dramatic rescues from the brink of despair or ruin. But all of them spoke a common theme—that Dolphus and the rest of the Mendenhall Ministries team had treated them with genuine compassion at their point of need.

That made a lasting impression on me. Having grown up in the church, I've seen too many organizations and ministries promise the moon, only to deliver moonbeams. So it was refreshing to find a group—one that had committed to some very modest goals and operated under less than ideal circumstances—actually delivering an impressive array of resources and services all out of proportion to its size or sophistication. This ministry was different. I tried to figure out why.

The easiest and most obvious explanation was Dolphus himself. I don't think any organization can ever be better than the quality of its leadership. And in Dolphus Weary, Mendenhall Ministries enjoys an unusually qualified leader. Some leaders dream dreams but never translate them into the right kind of action. Others are big on programs and pert charts but never notice the forest of opportunity because they lose themselves among the trees of detail. Dolphus is blessed with a healthy dose of vision married to a bias for action. It's been the right blend for the situation at Mendenhall.

But Dolphus's leadership alone couldn't explain what I found there. I looked carefully for signs of a personality cult but couldn't detect any. So I decided that other factors had to be involved. Eventually I discovered three crucial commitments that Dolphus had made; three values that, in my view, ultimately account for the impact the ministry is having on Simpson County. The first is his commitment to community. I don't mean just to the town of Mendenhall, though obviously he has committed to that. But rather a commitment to the concept of community, to creating a body of people willing to live out their lives together and, in the process, accomplish great and meaningful tasks together.

Dolphus has certainly been the most visible member of that community, since he serves as the ministry's head and travels extensively to represent it publicly. But if you visit Mendenhall, you will find an entire team of people carrying out the vision. We've mentioned several of them in this book, such as Pastor Artis Fletcher of Mendenhall Bible Church, Suzanne Griggins of the law office, Dr. Dennis Adams of the health clinic, his wife, Judi, who was so strategic in the founding of Genesis One School, and Billy Craft, who works in administration. But there are many others, unknown to those of us on the outside, but nevertheless making a profound difference in the lives of countless folks across Mississippi. This book has concentrated on Dolphus's story, but their contributions could easily fill—and really deserve—a separate book.

I came to view this group as more than just a task force, however. I found it to be a true community in the New Testament sense that its members have dedicated themselves to God, to each other, and to helping each other become whole, healthy, Christlike persons. Many organizations employ the skills of members, yet ignore their inner life. The ministry at Mendenhall was striking in its attempt to nourish the spirit of each participant so that he or she would have something genuine to offer others in need. This value on the spiritual, inner life has resulted in mature, responsible people, not just a proliferation of well-intentioned programs.

But people-making and community development take a long time, longer than most people realize, and certainly longer than most people are willing to commit to. That's why I also was impressed by Dolphus's commitment to a long-term process of change and development. I suppose this might seem impractical in a world in which political, economic, and cultural forces move forward at the speed of light. But many aspects of life do not change so quickly. Poverty and its cycles of hopelessness do not vanish overnight. Neither does entrenched racial discrimination. Neither does resistance to the gospel, even if it can transform. Progress in areas like these cannot be measured in years alone, but in lifetimes.

As I studied Dolphus and the Mendenhall Ministries community, I was struck with their tough-minded awareness that accomplishing their vision will require a lifetime of effort and devotion. Indeed, rather than seeing their work as complete, they view it as just beginning. From my vantage point, I think their best days are yet ahead.

A third value that set Dolphus and the ministry apart was their commitment to the gospel and its implications. We've witnessed a century in which religious leaders have viciously debated whether the gospel is primarily a message of future hope or an agenda for present justice. If we should have learned anything, it's that the gospel is not either/or but both/and—both salvation *and* social action, a message of love and justice, with implications for both eternity and our current situation. I had rarely seen a ministry wield these twin prongs of Christ's message more skillfully than the community at Mendenhall.

Nor was Mendenhall Ministries simply a community development organization masquerading under the pretense of a religious ministry. Obviously community development occurs through the programs. But as we've tried to show in this book, community development is not enough. Certainly it solves some significant problems. But one of the foundations underlying Mendenhall Ministries is a conviction that a person's ultimate need is spiritual and therefore involves his or her relationship to God. As I examined the philosophy behind the organization, I found this belief driving everything. Behind each program, including those involving community development, was a set of biblical principles—and a whole lot of prayer.

By the time Gary and I had shot our last tape and packed for the trip home, I realized that Mendenhall Ministries was something very special, a rare model of Christians functioning effectively as a spiritual community in a way that was transforming the larger, surrounding community. I also had come to respect Dolphus a great deal, both as a person and for what he had accomplished in his hometown.

As he drove us up to the airport at Jackson, he described for me his vision for the ministry. "Someday I'd like to see us serve as a model," he told me. "I'd like for us to inspire people all over the country—in Dallas, Chicago, Denver, everywhere—to use whatever resources God has given them to address the needs of poor people in their own communities."

Months later I was still reflecting on that comment, feeling personally challenged by it. What was I doing for the poor in my community? What part of myself was I giving away out of Christlike compassion?

One day Dolphus and I were chatting on the phone about a book I had just completed. A thought occurred to me. I said, "Dolphus, one of these days we need to get a book out about Mendenhall Ministries."

"We've already got one," he replied. This was news to me. But then he clarified the comment by adding, "I mean we've got a story that several people have been working on. But we don't know how to get it published."

"Dolphus, I know several publishers, and I know how to get a manuscript ready. I'd like to run with this project. I'd like to offer my help as my part in what you're trying to accomplish."

Later I learned that this idea had come as an answer to many prayers. But for me it was just a response to the challenge Dolphus had given on the way to Jackson—to use my resources on behalf of the poor. Many of us in the white community are so isolated from poverty that the only strategy we know for dealing with it is to throw money at it (a habit our government has schooled us in rather well). Certainly our money is needed. But through my encounter with Dolphus I came to see that I could make a more useful and wise investment by putting my skills as a writer into play.

How is a book about Dolphus going to help poor people in Mendenhall, or anywhere else? The answer has to do with the nature and value of writing and publishing. Stories like Dolphus's need to be heard, because they can inspire countless others to follow in his footsteps. A common longing I've heard among black leaders is for more role models, especially males, who embody the best of what it means to be black, to be human, and to be a man. I believe Dolphus can serve as such a model. So writing a book about him helps to publicize his example so that others can benefit.

The accomplishments of Mendenhall Ministries also need to be heard because they show us that no situation is so desperate that God's power and God's people and time cannot bring about change. Many whites today have come to regard the multitude problems of the poor as beyond hope. They simply throw up their hands in despair and cry, "Nothing can be done! It's hopeless! All we can do is contain the problem and, having done that, ignore it." I think Dolphus's story refutes that sort of thinking. It offers us a positive model of a ministry to the poor that is working. Therefore we need to notice it, affirm it, and, most important, learn from it. It challenges anyone who reads it to stop and consider: *What is my response to the poor in my locale? What resources do I have that could be exercised in some way on their behalf?*

I must add a final reason why I got involved in this project: I wanted to get to know Dolphus. I had seen the ministry, I had met the man, and I liked what I saw. I felt that a friendship had started. But I was intrigued: Where had this person come from? What explained him? Why would a black guy who grew up in Mississippi in the 1950s and 1960s go back and work in the very place that had caused him so much pain? I hope this book answers that question. If nothing else, I've had the benefit of deepening my knowledge of and friendship with one of the most impressive individuals I've ever known. Helping to write his story has been a privilege I will always treasure.

APPENDIX:
ABOUT MENDENHALL MINISTRIES

Mendenhall Ministries is a nonprofit, nondenominational Christian organization whose purpose is to minister to the total needs of people in the poor, rural areas of south central Mississippi. In its work it tries to model for others programs and services that can be replicated in other communities across the country. Emphasized in all the ministry's activities is the critical relationship between spiritual development and the struggle of the poor for self-sufficiency. Among the resources offered are:

THE HEALTH CENTER
More than 8,000 people each year use the services provided by Mendenhall Clinic, which has operated since the early 1970s. A full-time physician, nurse, and staff of four provide quality health and medical care primarily to low-income and uninsured people.

THE COMMUNITY LAW OFFICE
Combining professional legal expertise and Christian compassion, this program offers legal assistance and education to low-income people in Simpson County and surrounding counties. A full-time staff of five handles nearly 300 cases each year.

One of the Law Office's most innovative programs is the Interphasor Training Program. This program trains lay leaders at local churches in ways to address legal issues in their own communities.

GENESIS ONE CHRISTIAN SCHOOL
Originally started as a kindergarten in 1977, Genesis One School has developed into an impressive grade school combining sound academic instruction with teaching about the Bible and spiritual values. The goal of the school is to equip children academically for their future education and to

prepare them personally to become leaders in the Mendenhall community.

RECREATION PROGRAM
The aim of Mendenhall Ministries' recreation resources is to provide wholesome activities in an environment of Christian witness. A full-time staff person and several volunteers oversee programs for youth at the R. A. Buckley Center, in which more than a hundred kids participate weekly. This number doubles during the summer months.

ADULT EDUCATION
Three part-time instructors and several volunteers teach a variety of subjects and offer tutoring to enable local residents to acquire job skills, pass their GED exams, or participate in continuing education. Since its inception in 1974, the programs have helped more than 200 people.

THE COOPERATIVE FARM
Mendenhall Ministries owns and operates a 120-acre farm that includes three houses, forty head of cattle, and a peach orchard. A wide variety of crops are grown to provide for the physical needs of people in the Mendenhall community. The farm also seeks to demonstrate to local landowners that farming can subsidize their income.

The farm occasionally offers outreach programs to farmers throughout Simpson County. For example, one program used twenty sows to start eight farmers on small feeder pig operations.

THE THRIFT STORE
The ministry's Thrift Store provides quality merchandise at an affordable price to residents of Simpson County and surrounding counties. The store is strategically placed to be accessible to members of both the white and black communities.

Through careful acquisitions, purchasing, and management, the Thrift Store is completely self-supporting and employs four people full-time. More than 9,000 customers use the store each year, about half of whom are low income.

164

RADIO MINISTRY

Two part-time volunteers produce a weekly radio program aired on three stations covering a large portion of Mississippi. The purpose is primarily evangelistic. Through letters and other feedback, the ministry has discovered that both blacks and whites listen regularly, and a number have responded positively to the gospel presentations.

THE PASTOR'S DEVELOPMENT MINISTRY

Organized by Mendenhall Bible Church pastor Artis Fletcher in 1986, this program serves local churches by training pastors in biblical theology and practical skills for ministry. Local pastors attend monthly, and pastors from around the state attend quarterly seminars.

This program serves as a national training and resource support center for the Institute for Black Family Development, using audio and videotapes to establish training sites around the country. More than a hundred pastors and their wives from all across the United States have come for training.

CHRISTIAN YOUTH LEADERSHIP DEVELOPMENT

From its earliest days, Mendenhall Ministries has placed a value on leadership development, particularly among young people. This commitment translates into a program of training and experience for youth in Mendenhall designed to cultivate their leadership skills. Since its beginning in the late 1960s, more than 250 youth have participated, and 95 percent of them have gone on to skilled employment. About 20 percent have become staff persons in ministries such as Mendenhall Ministries. Dolphus and Rosie Weary are themselves products of this program.

VOLUNTEER SERVICES

This program is a way of providing cross-cultural experience to hundreds of nonlocal individuals and groups who desire to minister to the poor in a meaningful, practical way. Volunteers are used to tutor, to remodel buildings and houses, to build fences, and to carry out other projects benefiting the poor in Simpson County. A full-time coordinator oversees these visits.

Since 1968, more than 3,000 people from around the world have participated in this popular program. Churches in particular have found it to be a useful way of broadening the horizons and understanding of their people.

TECHNICAL ASSISTANCE AND SUPPORT

Because of its history and experience in Christian-based community development, Mendenhall Ministries is frequently called upon to help other organizations and groups develop programs and troubleshoot problems. This assistance includes on-site consulting and occasional conferences. In addition, Dolphus Weary represents Mendenhall Ministries by sitting on the boards of groups in: Poughkeepsie, New York; Memphis; Chicago; Covington, Louisiana; Dallas; Denver; Palo Alto, California; and Seattle.

OTHER PROGRAMS

Mendenhall Ministries carries out numerous other programs and activities, and over the years has participated in numerous projects related to its mission, including: the establishment of the first Head Start program in Simpson County, which continues to this day; the opening of a cooperative store that operated for eight years; the establishment of a cooperative housing facility of ten units for low-income families; the founding of the Simpson County Land Fund, which helps black landowners save their land; and the provision of technical assistance and office space for the new Simpson County Community Credit Union.

Mendenhall Ministries is a member of the Evangelical Council for Financial Accountability.

For more information about Mendenhall Ministries, write:

Mendenhall Ministries
P. O. Box 368
Mendenhall, MS 39114